Trade Wins or Trade Wars

Bogna Gawrońska-Nowak • Piotr Lis
Joanna Konieczna-Sałamatin

Trade Wins or Trade Wars

The Perceptions and Knowledge in the Free Trade Debate

palgrave
macmillan

Bogna Gawrońska-Nowak
Institute of Urban and Regional Development
Warsaw, Poland

Piotr Lis
Coventry University
Coventry, UK

Joanna Konieczna-Sałamatin
University of Warsaw
Warsaw, Poland

ISBN 978-3-030-76996-3 ISBN 978-3-030-76997-0 (eBook)
https://doi.org/10.1007/978-3-030-76997-0

This Palgrave Pivot imprint is published by the registered company Springer Nature Switzerland AG.
The registered company address is: Gewerbestrasse 11, 6330 Cham, Switzerland

Acknowledgements

We would like to express our appreciation to Agnieszka Karlińska from Faculty of Sociology, University of Warsaw, for opening our eyes to the world of digital text analysis and Clarin Project and to Jan Kocoń and Bartłomiej Piotr Bojanowski from Department of Computational Intelligence, Wrocław University of Science and Technology, who helped us with text analyses using their freshly created new tool.

About the Book

This book tackles the disconnect between social perceptions and expert knowledge regarding trade policy decisions. Using a Polish language internet database, the authors shed light on areas that need to be addressed when considering the adoption of particular trade policies by applying content and statistical analysis to produce an easy to deploy measure of populism in digital media, the "Media Populism Ratio".

Defining a mismatch between social perception and expert knowledge may contribute to a better understanding of the controversies on free trade, as well as properly defining possible sources of populism and social conflicts—therefore also revealing some potential weaknesses in the trade policy implementation level which are at times neglected or underestimated. The book will be relevant to students and researchers interested in economic policy, economic narratives, and cultural economics.

Contents

About the Authors

Bogna Gawrońska-Nowak is an associate professor and Head of the EURDATA (Data Science) Department at the Institute of Urban and Regional Development, Warsaw, Poland. She was a fellow and visiting researcher at the University of Padua and the University of Glasgow. She has expertise in using multidisciplinary quantitative research methods with a special focus on modelling instabilities and measuring policy effectiveness. She was consulting macroeconomic aspects of the Comprehensive Economic and Trade Agreement (CETA) implementation in Poland for the European Commission Representation in Poland. She has been a senior researcher and principal investigator in various research projects co-financed by well-recognised institutions: the National Bank of Poland, the National Centre for Research and Development in Poland, and the European Commission. Her current research agenda and her research-led teaching focus on the study of public opinion dynamics and social representations and the development of research methods based on the Citizen Science approach.

Piotr Lis is an economist with interests in political economy as well as armed conflict and security studies. He completed his PhD in Economics at Royal Holloway, University of London, UK, and is employed as Associate Professor of Economics at Coventry University, UK. He is also an associate member of the Research Centre for Financial and Corporate Integrity at Coventry.

His research incorporates elements of economics, political science, and international relations; for example, he studied the sensitivity of public opinion to war-related costs and terrorism. His recent projects analyse the impact of economic sanctions on target countries; linkages between terrorism, conflict, and foreign aid; and targeting of civilians in conflicts in Africa.

Joanna Konieczna-Sałamatin is a sociologist and an associate professor at the Faculty of Sociology, University of Warsaw, Poland. She combines interests in social sciences methodology and data analysis techniques with studying values and identities in Eastern Europe. Her research focuses on values shared in societies; she is a member of the Polish team of European Values Study. She is the author of articles on Polish and East-European societies, among which there were *The East of the West, or the West of the East? Attitudes toward the European Union and European Integration in Poland after 2008.* (with Maja Sawicka), "*East European Politics and Societies: And Cultures*". (2020, https://doi.org/10.1177/0888325420926633) and *The meaning of democracy: diverse understandings of the concept of democracy in Poland and other European societies.* "*Polish Sociological Review*". 1/214, 2021.

Abbreviations

CEE	Central and Eastern Europe
CEFTA	Central European Free Trade Agreement
CETA	Comprehensive Economic and Trade Agreement, sometimes referred to as the Canada–Europe Trade Agreement
CLARIN	Common Language Resources and Technology Infrastructure
DVA	domestic value added
EKD	Expert Knowledge Dictionary (constructed in Chap. 5)
EU	European Union
EVS	European Values Survey
FTA	Free Trade Agreement
FVA	Foreign value added
GATT	General Agreement on Tariffs and Trade
GVC	Global Value Chain(s)
LEM	Literary Exploration Machine (an NLP tool for Polish language)
NAFTA	North American Free Trade Agreement
NLP	Natural Language Processing
TPP	Trans-Pacific Partnership
TTIP	Transatlantic Trade and Investment Partnership
UNCTAD	United Nations Conference on Trade and Development
USMCA	United States–Mexico–Canada Agreement
WTO	World Trade Organization

List of Figures

List of Tables

CHAPTER 1

Introduction

Abstract This chapter is an introduction to the entire book content. We explain our motivation and inspiration by referring to the literature. Objectives, hypothesis, and assumptions of our work are presented.

Keywords Economic mindset • Online discussion on FTA • Social controversies • Sentiments towards free trade

Economists and policymakers' approach to trade is usually based on David Ricardo's nineteenth-century theory of comparative advantage according to which, as long as countries focus on what they are comparatively good at doing, trade is a win-win situation enabling both trading partners to enrich themselves. This leads to the conclusion that opening country borders, removing trade barriers, and leaving things to the assumed superior efficiency of free international markets are good for people's economic wellbeing. Nonetheless, this conviction lacks deeper insights into the complexity of both international and domestic economies. It does not tell us how gains from trade are distributed among economic participants and it is the fairness of that distribution or redistribution that is likely to drive people's attitudes towards free trade.

Trade liberalisation, tariff reductions, removal of non-tariff barriers, and Free Trade Agreements (FTAs) among countries have been a dominant strategy of the economic policy of developed and developing

B. Gawrońska-Nowak et al., *Trade Wins or Trade Wars*,
https://doi.org/10.1007/978-3-030-76997-0_1

countries for at least 40 years. The end of the Cold War, the bankruptcy of central planning, and the ensuing shift to the market economy of countries within the Soviet bloc[1] gave an additional impetus to globalisation as the former bloc members, representing over 400 million citizens, started integrating into the global economy. Many of those countries, including Poland, are now considered open economies. Nonetheless, economic openness has proven to be a controversial and hotly debated topic, both in developed and in emerging economies. An example of that debate in the former group is the narrative surrounding the North American Free Trade Agreement (NAFTA), which has caused major controversy in American politics for many years since it was first signed in 1993. Hillary Clinton called it a mistake during her Democratic primary election campaign in 2008 (NBC News 2008); also Barack Obama appeared sceptical towards the deal and wanted to renegotiate it (The Guardian 2009). The American public opinion perceived NAFTA as a factor contributing to unemployment and erosion of living standards among its middle class. Arguably, this sentiment led to the lack of enthusiasm in the US Congress for the Transatlantic Trade and Investment Partnership (TTIP), which was pursued by President Obama (Irwin 2015). However, it was the presidency of Donald Trump that marked America's turn towards the protectionist trade policy. President Trump withdrew the US from the Trans-Pacific Partnership (TPP), the ambitions for the Transatlantic Trade and Investment Partnership (TTIP) were largely scaled down by both the US and the EU, still little progress was achieved, and he threatened to withdraw from NAFTA if the agreement was not renegotiated. Under pressure, the signatories of NAFTA agreed on a new deal, the United States–Mexico–Canada Agreement (USMCA) which replaced NAFTA in 2020.[2]

In Kate Raworth's words, "economics [in particular political economy] is a mother tongue of public policy, the language of public life, and the mindset that shapes society" (Raworth 2017, p.6). That "tongue" tells and shapes the world through driving our thoughts, actions, and feelings which are often rooted in economic beliefs, values, and assumptions. In the Anthropocene era, this impact goes beyond our human world

[1] The Soviet or Eastern Bloc included the following countries: Albania, Bulgaria, Czechoslovakia, Hungary, East Germany, Poland, Romania, the Soviet Union, and Yugoslavia.

[2] For more details, see https://ustr.gov/usmca.

(society) as humanity's actions strongly influence the functioning of the natural world too. Therefore, it is crucial to understand how this economic language, driven by knowledge, models, and expert debates, is perceived by the public. We need to be able to read and understand the feelings, emotions, cognitive processes, and actions taken by the public in response to this economic language if we want to steer the economy and the world towards some goal.

The belief in the strong influence of economists on society has been shared by economists of various schools of thought over the years, including John Maynard Keynes who noted that "the world is ruled by little else" than "the ideas of economists and political philosophers" (Keynes 1961, p. 383). Friedrich von Hayek made a similar observation in his Noble Prize acceptance speech when saying "the influence of the economist that mainly matters is an influence over laymen: politicians, journalists, civil servants and the public generally" (von Hayek 1974). Thus, the gravity of the influence that economists and their theories hold over the world may have been recognised within the profession for quite some time, but how is the influence of economists' knowledge perceived in modern media and among their "laymen" readers?

This book is our modest attempt at answering this question in the context of international trade and Free Trade Agreements. We consider the voices of three groups of participants in the public debate: academic experts actively researching the subject of international trade, journalists whose role is to inform the society, and lay citizens expressing their views online. We focus our attention on the online discussions surrounding seven FTAs that took place in Poland since the mid-1990s. While solutions and recommendations proposed by experts should inform policymakers on pursuing deals that promote sustainable economic growth and, ideally, do not leave behind considerable pockets of society, we argue that expert views and knowledge should also find their reflection in the content of popular news outlets. The role of such media, and journalists writing the content, is to inform and educate the society, provide citizens with facts that enable them to develop views, and make decisions regarding their personal life, work, and political choices. To achieve this, the news and media content "served" to citizens must be rooted in factual information, knowledge, and, at least to some extent, critical analysis originating from experts on the subject. Thus, in this book, we set out to investigate how much of what is published online in Polish popular news outlets on the topic of free trade shows signs of containing expert knowledge, what sentiment and emotions does the content convey, and, finally, what makes media populist.

We also pay attention to the readers' comments posted in response to journalists' texts. Understating the views of the general public, their emotions and ways in which they engage with the expert knowledge content are equally important. In democratic countries, the public elects the government, consumes fruits of free trade but also pays its price, so it is crucial they understand the implication of any FTA for the country, society, economy, as well as personal economic circumstances. From the policymakers' perspective, an unfavourable public mood might derail or delay trade deals, as was seen in the Comprehensive Economic and Trade Agreement (CETA) debacle in Belgium, and the uninformed public is unlikely to express positive sentiment towards deals that appear to them as secretive, murky, or simply are not well understood. Unchecked free trade often creates winners and losers, and society as a whole should decide how the latter group ought to be compensated in order to achieve economic stability and social cohesion. We believe that to facilitate such decisions, and escape the trap of populism, citizens should be adequately informed about the gains and losses caused by FTAs. This brings us back to the importance of understanding how the public engages with information about free trade—a reliable diagnosis of the degree of knowledge and emotions present in the public debate can show policymakers (and experts) how much work needs to be done to inform and educate the public and helps to identify which aspects of trade should be explained better.

This book is a presentation of our research on the sentiments towards free trade contained in expert discourses and non-expert opinions conducted during the period 2016–2020, which was marked by increasing scepticism towards free trade among politicians and public opinion around the world. An important motivation for this work was the observed polarisation of views towards globalisation and trade. We note that large parts of the non-expert discussion ignore objective expert views, analysis, and facts but instead are based on hearsay and subjective emotions. This is worrying because ignoring or rejecting expert voices in the discourse may have harmful consequences for the society and economy, leading to instability, social conflicts, erroneous political decisions, economic inefficiency (reduced wealth), and provide ground for the ascendance of populists to power.

The structure of our book is as follows. In Chap. 2, we present the latest trends in free trade from a global perspective and introduce the essence of selected FTAs, which we later analyse in empirical chapters. Chapter 3 contains a compilation of our thoughts on the various driving forces that may have shaped major media narratives and collective perceptions of FTAs. In Chap. 4, we compare the Polish society to its international peers to determine the extent to which FTA attitudes are country-specific, and to what extent they fit and connect with the pan-European perspectives. Chaps. 5, 6 and 7 cover our empirical research results, the main purpose of which is to analyse the content and nature of the online FTAs debate. We find what the relationship between the expert knowledge content and the emotion-driven content in digital media is. In the final chapter, Chap. 8, we propose the Media Populism Ratio as a synthetic summary of our considerations.

References

Irwin, D.A., 2015, Free trade under fire, Princeton University Press, p. 2.

Keynes, J.M. (1961) The general theory of employment, interest and money. London, Macmillan, p. 383.

NBCNEWS.com, Clinton would fix husband's NAFTA mistakes, 14 Apr 2008, URL: http://www.nbcnews.com/id/24110966/ns/politics-decision_08/t/clinton-would-fix-husbands-nafta-mistakes/

Raworth, K. (2017). Doughnut economics: seven ways to think like a 21st-century economist. Chelsea Green Publishing, p. 6.

The Guardian, Obama raises NAFTA renegotiation during first official visit to Canada, 19 Feb 2009, URL: https://www.theguardian.com/world/2009/feb/19/barack-obama-stephen-harper-canada-visit

von Hayek, Friedrich (1974) Friedrich von Hayek, Banquet Speech upon acceptance of the Nobel-Prize, The Nobel Foundation, 10 December 1974

CHAPTER 2

Free Trade or Trade Wars: Retrospective Worldview

Abstract This chapter provides a compact guided tour through a careful selection of facts and figures of international trade. We highlight the developments, trends, and tendencies which appear critical for creating narratives that are spread within the public domain. We also present a brief description of the FTAs referenced in our empirical material presented in Chaps. 5, 6, and 7.

Keywords Globalisation • Free trade • GVC • FTA

A slowdown in the growth of global trade has been visible since 2011 and, most likely, has been associated with the decreasing demand for trade-intensive goods and increased protectionism. This trend may have been exacerbated by the COVID-19 pandemic which exposed the weaknesses of the global supply chains in delivering essential medical and personal protection supplies in 2020. In this chapter, we ask the question of what is international trade about today. Is it still about "*the highly fragmented pattern of production and trade in tasks*", rather than "*arm's-length exchanges of final goods or transfers within multinational corporations*" (Mayer et al. 2017, p. 3)?

This chapter provides a compact guided tour through a careful selection of facts and figures of international trade. We will highlight the

B. Gawrońska-Nowak et al., *Trade Wins or Trade Wars*,
https://doi.org/10.1007/978-3-030-76997-0_2

developments, trends, and tendencies which appear critical for creating narratives that are spread within the public domain. We also present a brief description of the FTAs referenced in our empirical material presented in Chaps. 5, 6, and 7.

2.1 International Trade Map: Challengers and Defenders

The trade in intermediate inputs accounts for as much as two-thirds of all international trade, and a significant share of trade passes through the Global Value Chains (GVCs), although the GVC share in global trade appears to have stagnated in recent years. GVC trade grew rapidly in the 1900s, but stagnated after the 2008 global financial crisis (The World Bank 2020).

Outsourcing and offshoring of production have resulted in the creation of a new global map of specialisation. GVCs have become crucial to understand the new complex set-up of value creation, retention, and capture (Gawrońska-Nowak 2019). Some world economy actors have benefited from the production defragmentation, while others have failed to integrate into GVCs successfully. Enabling free imports and exports as an entry pass to GVCs has not turned out to be sufficient in many cases.

Tracing the production fragmentation on the world map is not an easy task. The data released by UNCTAD (2018) show that the share of Foreign Value Added (FVA)[1] in exports was extremely high for the European Union in 2017 (38%). It was the highest among all developed economies (average: 32%) and higher than FVA in developing economies (average: 28%).

However, such a distinguished position in the FVA ranking may largely be explained by the advanced European integration processes, including

[1] Exports can be broken down into two categories: a domestic value added (**DVA**) component and a foreign value added (FVA) component. DVA is created through own, domestic factors of production. **FVA** corresponds to the value added of inputs that were imported in order to produce intermediate or final goods/services to be exported. Moreover, there are **upstream** and **downstream** links in international production chains. The country that supplies intermediate goods for further export by other countries is an upstream producer. A downstream producer is a country with a high import content in its exports. For more detailed information see WTO "Trade in Value-Added and Global Value Chains" profiles, Explanatory Notes: https://www.wto.org/english/res_e/statis_e/miwi_e/Explanatory_Notes_e.pdf.

markets and shared institutional settings, which encourage and support the rise of strong regional value chains. On the one hand, the process of further fragmentation of supply chains was related to the successful enlargement of the EU to include the Central and Eastern European (CEE) countries, which strengthened and developed networks of established producers—the old EU members. On the other hand, these established producers were actively changing their gravity directions, significantly increasing their trade contacts with the Asian countries, China and India in particular.

In addition to Belgium and the Netherlands, as well as the European Union in general, being located at the top positions of the exporting economies' list, EU countries occupied seven out of ten top places in the 2017 ranking of economies by their GVC participation rate, located higher than the United States, Japan, and developing economies (UNCTAD 2018).

Belgium and the Netherlands are global service, technology, and finance providers, and they have managed to go far beyond their own small domestic market capacities overcoming Singapore and China in the country rankings. It is worth noticing that even the biggest global production value-added providers still considerably depend on foreign inputs.

Poland's relatively high position in this ranking is worth noting. The country, along with other countries of CEE, joined GVCs in quite a spectacular way. Both forward and backward participation[2] has significantly improved economic upgrading in most of these countries. Between 1990 and 2015, their transformation processes also included a marked advance of their integration in GVCs. In particular, Poland and the Czech Republic experienced rapid growth.

Poland's promotion to the "advanced manufacturing and services" category means, following the methodology adopted by The World Bank (2020, pp. 22–23), that its share of manufacturing and business services in total domestic value-added exports was greater than 80%. The Czech Republic was doing even better, included in the category of "innovative activities". Thus, its intellectual property receipts were greater than 0.15% of GDP, and its R&D expenditures were greater than 1.5% of GDP.

[2] **Backward GVC participation** means that an economy imports intermediates to produce its exports. **Forward GVC participation** captures the domestic value added contained in inputs sent to third economies for further processing and export through value chains. For more detailed information see WTO "Trade in Value-Added and Global Value Chains" profiles, Explanatory Notes: https://www.wto.org/english/res_e/statis_e/miwi_e/Explanatory_Notes_e.pdf.

In fact, the Czech Republic stands out as the ten countries' regional CEE leader regarding investment in knowledge-based capital. The literature shows that it is precisely the investments in intangible assets (including the development of databases, software, science, engineering, design, managerial skills, etc.) that can provide the country with an upstream move in the GVCs hierarchy. The actual dynamics of CEE roles in the GVCs is very much different from their status quo in the 1990s. The CEE countries "debuted" in GVCs as new satellites of the big production centres from the EU. The old member states let new cells into their blood circulation to minimise labour costs, increase production efficiency, and look for new sources of competitive advantages, which determined geographical shifts in their supply chains. The Polish case study can serve as a success story that dates back to 1992 when General Motors Poland was established to import Opel cars to the absorptive Polish market. Ultimately, intensive cooperation with the Polish suppliers of vehicle parts resulted in significant company development, which contributed to the transformation of Poland's role in GVCs.

Meantime, between 1995 and 2008, the DVA content dropped from 79% to 66%, while FVA share increased from 21% to 34% in the German car industry sector. The intermediates were increasingly imported in Germany, generating income for labour and capital employed outside the country. Additionally, it can be noticed that the value added by capital increased while the share of labour dropped. The drop in labour was almost exclusive for less-skilled workers inside the country. The share of high-skilled workers both within and outside of Germany increased. As Timmer et al. (2014, p. 104) say: "*the patterns of shifting location and factor content of activities in the global value chain of German cars are representative for many other chains of manufactures*". Changes in factor shares in the GVCs observed between 1995 and 2008 in "old" Europe can be perceived as signalling for the decline of manufacturing, that is shrinking labour demand of low-skilled workers inside the country and in consequence their income cuts. France experienced a decrease of low-skilled workers share by 8.7%, UK by 8%, Italy by 14.8%, and Spain by 12.9%, which is confirmed by a wider trend (WTO 2019).

Criscuolo and Timmis (2018) use centrality metrics to identify central sectors and countries, that is highly connected and influential within GVCs and peripheries, that is sectors and countries weakly connected within GVCs. Their analysis covers 62 economies for the period between 1995 and 2011. Their findings contribute to a better understanding of the consequences of industrial district traditional model evolution in the EU signalled earlier by Timmer et al. (2014). As a matter of fact, there are some new centres of world manufacturing established although some remained unchanged. Computer and electronics manufacturing nerves have been moved to emerging economies of Asia, while the UK and Japan have suffered from declining importance.

Moreover, almost every manufacturing industry in the UK and Italy has become less influential. However, Germany and the US have retained their leading roles as motor vehicle, machinery, and equipment manufacturing hubs. At the same time, CEE economies have been gradually gaining more influential positions, advancing their connections with high-developed economies like Germany.

Another interesting finding is about shock propagation mechanism. A minority of firms and sectors that are highly connected by GVCs account for a majority of aggregate volatility. For example, in Belgium, 100 most central firms account for 91.3% of Belgian aggregate volatility (Magerman et al. 2016). A shock affecting a company has multidimensional consequences. Not only suppliers and customers of that company are hit but also suppliers and customers of its suppliers and customers. This process is replicated worldwide in the whole network of GVCs. Hence the central firms, industries, and countries "*play a disproportionate role in determining aggregate performance*" (Criscuolo and Timmis 2018, p. 6). Mitigating supply shock is one of the trade-offs that the firm may face, that is higher production costs and lower productivity versus lower risk.

To an extent, the decline of manufacturing in advanced economies could be neutralised by reshoring, that is moving back of the value chains to the multinational firms' home economies. Such a trend is very much in line with the postulate that the economy's openness runs counter to its resilience. That approach has gained ample attention in the face of the shocks and risks associated with the COVID-19 pandemic threats. However, relying on the surveys exploring intentions of managers, one may say that the "coming back" trend is undeniably apparent, but judging on what firms have already done, the prospects seem to be less optimistic.

2.2 How Free Is International Trade Today?

Since 2011 production fragmentation has ceased substantially. It is also true that a large portion of the global demand shifted to services that are less trade intensive than goods.[3] However, it is impossible to ignore the importance of trade wars and their role in shaping the "new view" of trade relations in the entire global economy. The tariffs imposed by the US and China on each other covered more than half of their bilateral trade in 2018. The impact force of protectionism was mainly directed at manufacturing (UNCTAD 2019).

It seems obvious that tensions among major economies have far-reaching (ripple) effects on the rest of the global economy. The balance of the profit and loss account depends largely on the extent to which goods "protected" now by the US and China can be substituted by the products delivered domestically or by foreign competitors. Considering this, the 2019 results of the Global Competitiveness Report (World Economic Forum 2019)[4] leave much to be desired in global competitiveness. The global competitiveness gap (measured as the distance to the frontier, which is an ideal and hypothetical situation where a country achieves the perfect score on every component of the index) stands at almost 40 points, which still seems a lot.

According to the UNCTAD estimates of the diversion effects, the EU countries are likely to increase their exports the most because of the US versus China trade tensions (UNCTAD 2019, p. 4). Additionally, imposing tariffs may encourage domestic relocalisation of GVCs.

The trade wars have changed the world scene a lot. They have caused the weakening of the multilateral trading system and moved trade negotiations and settlements out of the WTO domain, placing them at a bilateral level. Moreover, Hoekman (2020, p. 98) observes: "*A justification for the term 'war' is that US actions go beyond traditional measures such as anti-dumping, countervailing duties, and global safeguard actions by invoking national security as a justification for trade restrictions*". Rising use of trade-distorting policies is a part of the broader trend. Many measures that

[3] It must be noticed, however, that recently services sectors have been heavily affected by the COVID-19 pandemic. Especially tourism, transport, and distribution services have suffered as a result of mobility restrictions and social distancing measures. At the same time, demand for information and communication technology (ICT) services and related infrastructure has grown significantly in the pandemic.

[4] http://www3.weforum.org/docs/WEF_TheGlobalCompetitivenessReport2019.pdf.

various countries have imposed since 2009 deform trade and competition. Most of the policy instruments used for that purpose belong to the non-tariff category (see Table 2.1). Technical Barriers to Trade (TBT) constitute more than 30% of product lives and affect 70% of world trade, price control measures mark 15% of it, while Sanitary and Phytosanitary similarly 20%.

The sudden outbreak of COVID-19 has brought about harsh restrictions and a drastic fall in demand worldwide. As a result, trade experienced severe downturns, reflected in WTO goods barometer[5] performance.

Table 2.1 Measures initiated and in force from 2008 to 2019

	2008	*2009*	*2010*	*2011*	*2012*	*2013*	*2014*	*2015*	*2016*	*2017*	*2018*	*2019*
Sanitary and phytosanitary												
Initiated	587	522	704	685	546	652	832	1018	769	1001	1316	1223
In force	353	313	418	360	345	346	368	287	328	114	3	0
Technical bariers to trade												
Initiated	1235	1351	1266	1140	1479	1536	1428	1222	1443	1734	2041	1986
In force	49	254	291	225	236	207	194	469	452	223	112	142
Antidumping												
Initiated	197	204	171	164	195	262	230	221	277	246	195	100
In force	156	156	133	107	130	177	169	196	184	190	211	90
Countervailing												
Initiated	14	28	10	25	21	29	41	30	33	41	50	15
In force	11	9	19	10	10	13	12	14	26	18	28	18
Safeguards												
Initiated	8	21	18	10	22	18	18	15	20	7	18	28
In force	6	9	5	11	6	5	19	18	6	9	12	13
Special safeguards												
Initiated	11	16	20	24	17	17	2	0	0	0	0	0
In force	107	119	72	75	81	39	21	3	0	0	0	0
Quantitative restrictions												
Initiated	1	16	5	2	98	1	196	0	445	1	0	0
In force	107	119	72	75	81	39	21	3	0	0	0	0
Tariff quotes												
Initiated	0	0	0	0	0	0	0	0	0	0	0	0
In force	0	3	0	0	2	4	0	0	0	0	0	0
State trading enterprices												
Initiated	0	0	0	0	0	0	0	0	0	0	0	0
In force	1	1	1	0	0	1	15	26	0	0	1	0

Source: WTO database: https://www.wto.org/english/res_e/statis_e/statis_e.htm

[5] The WTO's Goods Trade Barometer provides real-time information on the trajectory of world trade relative to recent trends, see: https://www.wto.org/english/res_e/statis_e/wtoi_e.htm.

Right after the pandemic outbreak it showed a steep decline in global goods trade. It was very much in line with the WTO's trade forecast issued in April, which projected a decline in world merchandise trade between 13% and 32% in 2020. However, it must be noted that world trade was already slowing in 2019 before the COVID-19 outbreak, probably mostly due to persistent trade tensions and slowing economic activity in major economies. Good news is that in the fourth quarter of 2020 trade rebounded from a deep COVID-19 slump. It is hard to say whether that tendency will be continued in the longer perspective.

2.3 Seven Agreements

In the following chapters, we conduct a content and sentiment analysis of seven Polish internet portals and investigate the Polish public opinion attitudes towards seven trade agreements: CEFTA, CETA, GATT, NAFTA, TTIP, TPP, and WTO. Some of these agreements directly concern the Polish economy, so the Polish authorities have to choose whether to join and ratify them, while others, namely NAFTA and TPP, do not involve the Polish state but still have been hotly debated in the Polish media. We briefly discuss each of the agreements, pointing out their origins and key aspects.

The General Agreement on Tariffs and Trade (GATT) was first signed by 23 nations in 1947 and is by far the oldest of the analysed treaties. This multilateral agreement aimed at a "substantial reduction of tariffs and other barriers to trade and (…) elimination of discriminatory treatment in international commerce".[6] It followed several negotiation rounds over the decades eventually leading to the creation of the World Trade Organization (WTO) in 1994. As of 2020, WTO has 164 member states. Following the 1994 modifications, the GATT text is still in effect which probably explains why it is still frequently referred to in the expert and public discourse. Both GATT and WTO are assumed to have made a significant contribution to reducing both tariff and non-tariff barriers to trade. The average tariff level among GATT members in 1947 was estimated at 22%,[7] whereas

[6] World Trade Organization, The General Agreement on Tariffs and Trade (GATT 1947), Legal Texts, URL: https://www.wto.org/english/docs_e/legal_e/gatt47_01_e.htm.

[7] Bown, Chad P.; Irwin, Douglas A. (2015). "The GATT's Starting Point: Tariff Levels circa 1947". NBER Working Paper No. 21782.

in 2017 the weighted average tariff stood at only 2.59%.[8] The agreements provided several innovations that enhanced trade policy transparency, established ground for trade negotiations, reduced discriminatory practices in international trade, and consequently facilitated further reductions in trade barriers and peaceful resolution of bilateral trade disputes.[9]

The North American Free Trade Agreement (NAFTA) was established in 1994 as a trilateral trade bloc encompassing the United States, Canada, and Mexico with the total population of nearly half a billion people in 2018.[10] Although the agreement reduced trade barriers between the three countries, it was surrounded by a great deal of controversy from its inception, especially in the US and Canada. The US public opinion appeared divided in their assessments of NAFTA's effect on the US economy. According to a 2017 Gallup Poll, 48% of the public saw NAFTA as beneficial and 46% as detrimental to the US economy.[11] The controversy surrounded mostly three key issues: whether NAFTA was creating or destroying American jobs, its impact on the environment and immigration to the US.[12] Over the years, politicians on both sides of US politics vowed to renegotiate the deal. President Donald Trump branded it as "perhaps the worst trade deal ever made"[13] and pursued aggressive renegotiation. In 2018 the three countries reached an agreement to replace NAFTA with the new United States–Mexico–Canada Agreement (USMCA) which came into effect in July 2020.

The Central European Free Trade Agreement (CEFTA) is another regional trade agreement signed by Poland, Hungary, and Czechoslovakia (soon to become the Czech Republic and Slovakia) in 1992. The agreement came into force in 1994 and later was joined by Albania, Bosnia and Herzegovina, Bulgaria, Croatia, Moldova, Montenegro, North Macedonia,

[8] World Bank, URL: https://data.worldbank.org/indicator/TM.TAX.MRCH.WM.AR.ZS.

[9] Elsig, Manfred, Bernard Hoekman, and Joost Pauwelyn, eds. Assessing the World Trade Organization: Fit for Purpose?. Cambridge University Press, 2017.

[10] NAFTA was a successor to the 1988 Canada–United States Free Trade Agreement.

[11] Swift, Art (2017) Americans Split on Whether NAFTA Is Good or Bad for U.S., Gallup, URL: https://news.gallup.com/poll/204269/americans-split-whether-nafta-good--bad.aspx.

[12] Merolla, J., Stephenson, L. B., Wilson, C. J., & Zechmeister, E. J. (2005). Globalization, globalización, globalisation: Public opinion and NAFTA. Law & Bus. Rev. Am., 11, 573.

[13] White House, Remarks by President Trump on the United States–Mexico–Canada Agreement, 1 October 2018, URL: https://www.whitehouse.gov/briefings-statements/remarks-president-trump-united-states-mexico-canada-agreement/.

Romania, Serbia, Slovenia, and Kosovo.[14] One of the CEFTA's objectives was to facilitate the region's integration into the Western European political and economic institutions. Eight of the members, including the founding countries, have joined the European Union, which meant the end to their CEFTA membership. The agreement was modified in 2006 to reflect its changing structure and currently includes seven South-Eastern European countries with a total population of approximately 21.5 million inhabitants.[15] CEFTA states achieved full liberalisation of tariffs in manufacturing sectors and significantly reduced tariffs in agriculture, leading to significant increases in trade flows among CEFTA parties.[16] Intra-CEFTA exports accounted for 15% of all exports and just under 10% of all imports by CEFTA members in 2016.[17] Elimination of non-tariff barriers remains the current focus of the CEFTA member states.

The Comprehensive Economic and Trade Agreement (CETA), sometimes referred to as the Canada–Europe Trade Agreement, was signed between the European Union and Canada in 2016. The negotiation and ratification process caused a lot of controversies and captured a significant amount of media attention, especially the Walloon opposition's drama to the treaty made major headlines internationally.[18] As of 2020, the agreement is not fully in force yet; it is still pending ratification by all national legislatures of EU countries (Poland has not ratified it yet), but its parts have been provisionally applied. Supporters of CETA expect a significant increase in trade flows and employment thanks to reductions in tariffs, goods checks, non-trade barriers, levelling the playing field in the intellectual property rights, and an introduction of a new court system for investment dispute settlement.[19] The investor-state dispute settlement

[14] Represented by the United Nations Mission in Kosovo (UNMIK).

[15] The current CEFTA states are: Albania, Bosnia and Herzegovina, Moldova, Montenegro, North Macedonia, Serbia, and Kosovo.

[16] OECD (2012) Elimination of Non-Tariff Barriers in CEFTA, CEFTA Issues Paper 4, URL: https://www.oecd.org/south-east-europe/programme/cefta4.pdf.

[17] CEFTA (2016) CEFTA Trade Statistics 2016, URL: https://cefta.int/trade-info-centre/statistics/.

[18] McKenna, Barrie (2016) What's Wallonia's deal? A primer on its role in CETA's crisis, The Globe and Mail, 24 October 2016, URL: https://www.theglobeandmail.com/report-on-business/international-business/european-business/explainer-ceta-wallonia-europe-and-canada/article32489554/.

[19] European Commission (2017) Guide to the Comprehensive Economic and Trade Agreement (CETA), Publications Office of the European Union, URL: http://trade.ec.europa.eu/doclib/docs/2017/september/tradoc_156062.pdf.

(ISDS) mechanism appeared particularly controversial raising fears that large corporations could sue national governments for multibillion-dollar compensations should they think national policies are damaging their business.[20] CETA's critics also feared its negative impact on European consumer rights, food safety, unemployment, and environmental degradation.[21] We will pay particular attention to those issues when analysing experts' sentiment, journalists, and lay people towards CETA (Chaps. 5, 6, and 7).

The remaining two agreements, TTIP and TPP, have not reached a signing stage but attracted a lot of media attention and heated debate worldwide. The Transatlantic Trade and Investment Partnership (TTIP) between the European Union and the United States was the largest bilateral trade agreement ever negotiated.[22] The two parties jointly accounted for around half of the global GDP and had a combined market of around 800 million consumers. According to some estimates, the deal would boost the EU's GDP by 120 billion euro (0.5%) and the US by 95 billion euro (0.4%), creating several hundred thousand or even a million new jobs dependent on exports. However, not all analysts agreed with those assessments as other simulations showed that TTIP could lead to net losses in EU's GDP, personal incomes, and 600,000 jobs.[23] The negotiations, which started in 2013, ground to a halt under Donald Trump's presidency and ended without a conclusion in 2016. The Council of the European

[20] For examples of such criticism see: Mineur, Anne-Marie, (2019) Compatibility with EU law is not real issue with ISDS, EUObserver, 30 April 2019, URL: https://euobserver.com/opinion/144752; and EDRI (2015) Dutch civil rights group highlights dangers of ISDS in trade deals, European Digital Rights, 9 March 2015, URL: https://edri.org/dutch-civil-rights-group-highlights-dangers-isds/.

[21] Such voices are exemplified in: BBC News (2016) EU Commission refuses to revise Canada Ceta trade deal, BBC News, 23 September 2016, URL: https://www.bbc.co.uk/news/world-europe-37450742; Eberhardt, Pia, Blair Redlin and Cecile Toubeau (2014) Trading Away Democracy. How CETA's investor protection rules threaten the public good in Canada and the EU, multiple publishers, URL: https://www.tni.org/files/download/ceta-isds-en_0.pdf.

[22] Novotná, T., Telò, M., Morin, J. F., & Ponjaert, M. F. (Eds.). (2015). The politics of transatlantic trade negotiations: TTIP in a globalized world. Ashgate Publishing, Ltd.

[23] Kraatz, Susanne (2014). The Transatlantic Trade and Investment Partnership (TTIP) and Labour, Briefing, Employment and Social Affairs, European Parliament, URL: https://www.europarl.europa.eu/RegData/etudes/BRIE/2014/536315/IPOL_BRI(2014)536315_EN.pdf.

Union declared the TTIP negotiations "obsolete and no longer relevant"[24] three years later. The secrecy surrounding the negotiations became controversial in Europe,[25] adding to the deal's widespread criticism. This was not helped by multiple leaks which revealed that the EU was under pressure to weaken its stance on environmental protection, animal testing, consumer rights, public health, food safety standards and that the US was demanding American firms to be allowed a degree of input into the EU regulatory process similar to that enjoyed by the European firms.[26] These revelations heated the public debate.

Another agreement that has not come to fruition is the Trans-Pacific Partnership (TPP) which was signed by Australia, Brunei, Canada, Chile, Japan, Malaysia, Mexico, New Zealand, Peru, Singapore, Vietnam, and the United States on 4 February 2016 but did not come into effect. The US president Donald Trump withdrew his country from the agreement in January 2017, and the remaining 11 countries moved to sign a new agreement, Comprehensive and Progressive Agreement for Trans-Pacific Partnership, which became effective at the end of 2018. The main provisions of TPP aimed at lowering tariff and non-tariff barriers to trade as well as establishing an investor-state dispute settlement (ISDS) mechanism. Another oft-cited geopolitical aim was to integrate the participants more firmly into the US zone of influence and limit their economic dependence on China.[27] In its original form, TPP would form a major trading bloc among countries inhabited by 800 million people and responsible for a third of global trade, and 40% of world GDP,[28] which explains why it received so much attention worldwide, including in Poland.

[24] Council of the European Union (2019). Council Decision (EU) 6052/19. Brussels, 9 April 2019, URL: https://www.consilium.europa.eu/media/39180/st06052-en19.pdf.

[25] Boren, Zachary Davis (2015). TTIP controversy: Secret trade deal can only be read in secure 'reading room' in Brussels. The Independent, 14 August 2015, URL: https://www.independent.co.uk/news/world/europe/ttip-controversy-secret-trade-deal-can-only-be-read-secure-in-reading-room-in-brussels-10456206.html.

[26] Neslen, Arthur (2016). Leaked TTIP documents cast doubt on EU-US trade deal, The Guardian, 1 May 2016, URL: https://www.theguardian.com/business/2016/may/01/leaked-ttip-documents-cast-doubt-on-eu-us-trade-deal.

[27] Green, M. J., & Goodman, M. P. (2015). After TPP: the Geopolitics of Asia and the Pacific. The Washington Quarterly, 38(4), 19–34.

[28] Granville, Kevin (2016). The Trans-Pacific Partnership Trade Accord Explained, The New York Times, 26 July 2016; and BBC News (2015). Trans-Pacific free trade deal agreed creating vast partnership, BBC News, 6 October 2015, URL: https://www.bbc.co.uk/news/business-34444799.

Trade negotiations and trade agreements are important strategic instruments of geopolitics and economic policy and as such do not happen in a vacuum and may feed off each other as countries learn from previous experiences. For example, GATT, and later WTO, laid the ground for the negotiation and, in some cases, implementation of the other five agreements discussed in this book. Similarly, people's opinions and attitudes towards free trade in general and specific trade deals are likely to be shaped by their knowledge, understanding, and experience of earlier agreements and other aspects of international trade. The chronology of trade-related events confounds this further. As Fig. 2.1 shows, multiple trade deals may be negotiated, signed, and enacted or rejected within relatively short periods—2016 and 2017 are very good examples of that. We show that such periods are marked by heated debates among experts, journalists, politicians, and regular people (see Chaps. 5, 6, and 7), and the views or sentiment towards one FTA may be closely linked to an individual's perception of other FTAs. We expect those linkages to be stronger when such events are in close temporal proximity. Figure 2.1 puts the key events related to the seven discussed agreements in chronological order. We will refer back to that timeline when discussing our data and results in Chaps. 5, 6, and 7.

2.4 Summarising Remarks

The model of international trade has significantly changed in recent years. The development of GVCs, combined with the development of emerging economies, has created a new network of connections in the global economy and resulted in broadly understood socio-economic and political consequences. The CEEan countries have advanced in this network, while old Europe—stretching its spheres of influence within the regional GVCs. The changes have transformed European labour markets affecting the manufacturing workers in particular and fuelling populism.

Trade wars symbolically and literally started a new chapter in the history of globalisation marked by protectionism. The implementation of a new generation of FTAs, such as CETA and TTIP, has been slowed down and hampered. Only CETA finally "saw the light of day"; TTIP, with the decline of the era of dynamic development of globalisation, has remained frozen ever since. Additionally, the threat of the pandemic has further strengthened anti-globalisation trends.

Despite the arguably universal nature of the described trends, their manifestations are subject to differentiation—depending on the national

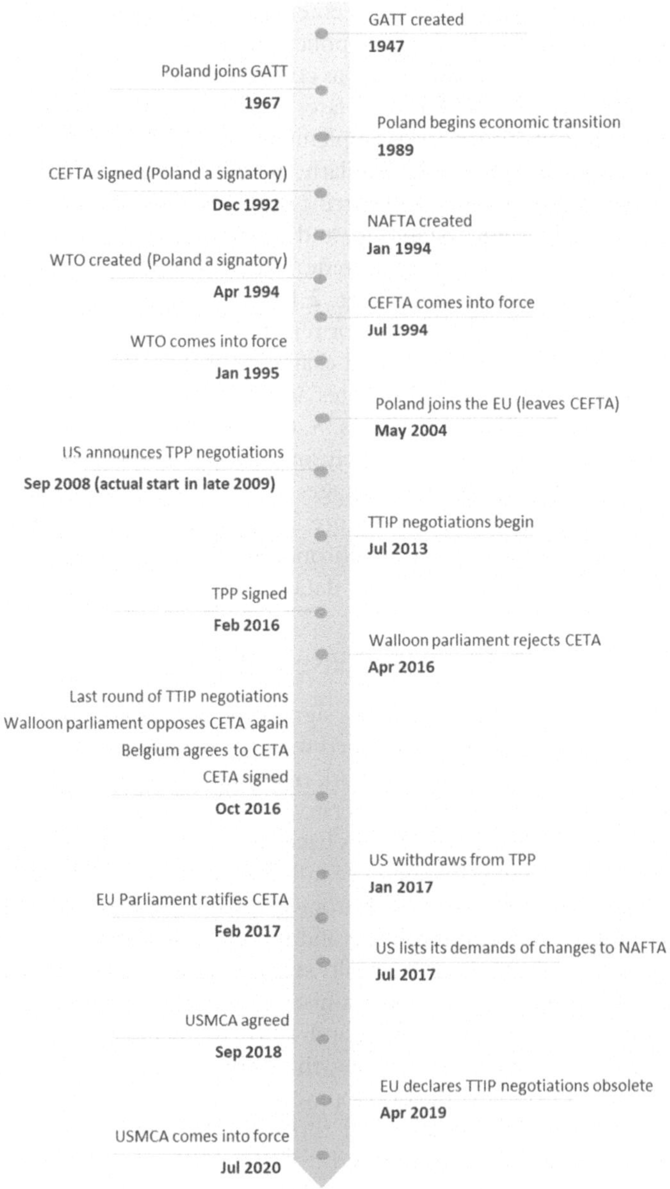

Fig. 2.1 Timeline of key events

context. Poland and other CEE countries should be carefully considered as moderate winners. However, the final profit and loss balance is not complete. Too many unknowns in this balance sheet still remain to be considered. The trade wars have made everyone aware of the seriousness of competition and tensions between China and the US, and more recently, other English-speaking countries. Meanwhile, the COVID-19 pandemic added to the domestic and global uncertainties, which are likely to be exacerbated even further by the accelerating climate change crisis. It is impossible to say with any serious degree of certainty what the future of the international trade holds. Will the global economy return onto the path of the accelerated integration and international trade interdependency or will the world turn its back on globalisation and undergo a phase of reverse globalisation?

References

Criscuolo, C., & Timmis, J. (2018). The changing structure of global value chains: Are central hubs key for productivity? International Productivity Monitor, 34, 64.

Gawrońska-Nowak, B. (2019). Is homo oeconomicus an extinct species, and does it matter for EUropean integration? Attitudes towards free trade and populism. Global Discourse: An Interdisciplinary Journal of Current Affairs, 9(1), 249–264.

Hoekman, B. (2020). Trade wars and the World Trade Organization: causes, consequences, and change. Asian Economic Policy Review, 15(1), 98–114.

Magerman, G., De Bruyne, K., Dhyne, E., & Van Hove, J. (2016). Heterogeneous firms and the micro origins of aggregate fluctuations (No. 312). NBB Working Paper.

Mayer, F. W., Phillips, N., & Posthuma, A. C. (2017). The political economy of governance in a 'global value chain world'. New Political Economy, 22(2), 129–133.

Timmer, M. P., Erumban, A. A., Los, B., Stehrer, R., & De Vries, G. J. (2014). Slicing up global value chains. Journal of Economic Perspectives, 28(2), 99–118.

UNCTAD (2018). World Investment Report. Investment and New Industrial Policies.

UNCTAD (2019). Key Statistics and Trends in Trade Policy 2018, Geneva.

World Bank (2020). World Development Report 2020: Trading for Development in the Age of Global Value Chains. Washington, DC: World Bank. © World Bank. https://openknowledge.worldbank.org/handle/10986/32437 License: CC BY 3.0 IGO.

World Economic Forum (2019). Global Competitiveness Report, 2019.

WTO (2019). Technological Innovation, Supply Chain Trade, and Workers in a Globalised World, Global Value Chain Development Report 2019.

CHAPTER 3

Free Trade or Trade Wars: Controversies, Political Interests, and Narratives

Abstract This chapter tries to capture both the factors that created "*the symbolic power*" and "*the symbolic efficacy*" (Bourdieu. Critique of Anthropology, 4[13–14], 77–85, 1979) of economists' narrative concerning international trade and map some critical factors of its transformation. First, we provide a brief overview of the theoretical concepts embedded in the economic mainstream that might explain what factors play a decisive role in shaping people's attitudes towards free trade. Second, we look critically at the "*economic consensus*". We seek to identify the importance of its coherence and erosion to the public discourse on free trade and outline the circumstances favouring either the coherence or the erosion of this economic narrative globally. We also list by name the "major players" in the global free trade debate. Finally, we try to capture the sounds of new tones that could prove to be dominant in post-consensus narratives.

Keywords Attitude towards trade • Economic consensus • Symbolic power of economics • Mapping transformations of International Trade

What makes Free Trade Agreements and international trade such controversial issues? The backlash against globalisation, and international trade in particular, is usually seen as rooted in the uneven distribution of trade gains. Foreign competition is perceived (and often truly works in this way)

B. Gawrońska-Nowak et al., *Trade Wins or Trade Wars*,
https://doi.org/10.1007/978-3-030-76997-0_3

by some economists and public opinion as a crowding-out mechanism, destructive for local industries and narrowly specialised labour demand. Negative trade effects might have made people vote for populists and, in Europe, question European integration.

While looking at the expert economic discourse in hindsight, one is likely to feel alarmed, even infuriated, and ask how it could happen that economists had not considered all the (implicitly negative) effects of international trade and, more broadly, globalisation. This question belongs to a broad trend to examine and contest economists' knowledge, models, theories, and judgements, including a critique of capitalism and the neoliberal or neoclassical economic thought. Regardless of the detailed assessment of the validity of this criticism, the current state of knowledge about globalisation (comprising international trade and FTAs) creates a more complex picture of the resulting interdependencies and connections, going beyond the interpretations formulated over the past few decades by the experts, kept mainly in the spirit of the mainstream economics.

In this chapter, we will try to capture both the factors that created "*the symbolic power*" of economists' narrative concerning the international trade and map some critical factors of its transformation. Undoubtedly, before the global financial crisis (GFC), several opinion-forming centres (intuitively labelled as Anglophone, US, Western culture oriented, and elitist) dominated the economic expert discourse. Simultaneously and gradually, the so-called peripheries and emerging voices (intuitively labelled as non-Anglophone, non-Western, anti-elitist) rejected the role of the passive recipients of the main message. They began to take over and develop the space of public debate actively. Their growing strength increased with the Chinese economy's power and the reshuffling of the map of trade connections. Massive social demand for new "*symbolic power*" and new "*symbolic efficacy*" has been born. We explain it in the remaining sections of this chapter using Bourdieu's concept (1979). These new circumstances have washed out the compact set of "economic consensus" views.

3.1 Attitudes Towards Trade

Brexit has been one of the key events in international trade in recent years or even decades. Studies have shown that the support for leaving the European Union was systematically higher in regions hit harder by import shocks (Colantone and Stanig 2018). The effect of import shock remains statistically significant, even after immigration variables are added. Los et al. (2017) conducted an analysis at the NUTS 2 level. Their results support the hypothesis about the relation between the Brexit "*Leave*" vote and local industries' dependency on the EU markets. The regions of the UK that depended the most on European markets displayed higher proportions of Leave voters.

Dippel et al. (2016) use causal mediation analysis to identify trade integration effects on voting behaviour in Germany. They focus on federal election data from 1987 to 2009 and UN Commodity Trade Statistics Database (Comtrade) for trade variables and German Social Security records as well as German Federal Statistical Office data for labour market variables. They find that extreme-right party vote share increases with import competition and decreases with export access opportunities. Two-thirds of the total effect of trade integration on voting is driven by labour market adjustments, mainly referring to manufacturing employment.

Dluhosch (2018) discovered that the level of the economy's openness changes the perception of income inequality. The higher the openness, the more people are concerned about the income gap. Dluhosch links that to the group identity based on the "*them-versus-us*" perspective on trade. She thinks that this type of attitude towards trade makes people more susceptible to populism than those motivated solely by the distributional impact of trade. Her arguments should be considered as empirical evidence for the existence of bias perception towards trade, which can be rooted in factors different from economic self-interest. It is worth noticing that these findings are in line with Mutz and Kim's (2017) analysis. Their survey experiment results support the perceived intergroup competition hypothesis promoted by Dluhosch (2018). A higher level of such competition leads some Americans to prefer beggar-thy-neighbour-policy, that is trade policies that benefit "*the in-group*" and hurt "*the out-group*".

There is a substantial amount of literature discussing the formation of attitudes towards free trade (Gawrońska-Nowak 2019). One of the vital cornerstones of that debate is the economic self-interest hypothesis whose origins can be traced to the Stopler-Samuelson theorem: "*regardless of the number of goods and factors, at least one factor of production must experience a decline in real income from trade as long as trade induces the relative price of some domestically produced good(s) to fall (and as long as the productivity benefits from trade are restricted to the traditional, inter-sectoral allocative efficiency improvements*)", Rodrik described on his weblog (2018).[1] Such reasoning implies that lay citizens are mainly interested in the consequences of free trade for themselves. Empirical studies exploring the economic self-interest hypothesis have been concentrated on job-related attributes such as skill levels, income, and employment sector. That direction of research is appealing to the "*winners or losers*" perspective. In this scenario, an individual employee's attitude towards free trade would be affected by his/her ability to adapt to a new market environment, which is much easier for a high-skilled worker. It is also quite possible that individuals working for the same industry may have diverging economic self-interests towards free trade, depending on their firms' productivity level.

The hypothesis of the socio-tropic formation of attitudes towards free trade contrasts with the economic cost-benefit assessment process rooted in an individualistic approach. Mansfield and Mutz (2009) noticed that the citizens' attitude formation depends on how they perceive free trade effects for the national economy rather than how they refer these effects to their own jobs and incomes. Socio-tropic hypothesis includes "*group clashes*", whereby individuals may form their attitudes towards trade by socialising and interacting with each other through their group-belonging patterns. Decisions to join any particular group are not random, and as an aware self-selection process, they must have an impact on free trade attitude. The survey experiment conducted by Lü et al. (2012) proves that both Chinese and American citizens want to protect the low-skilled workers due to some form of "*altruism*", at the same time they are likely to oppose protecting high-skilled (well paid) workers due to "envy" towards the rich. Thus, "altruism" and "elite aversion" have rebalancing power.

Information transmission from groups to individuals and among individuals and groups can be a crucial but still underestimated factor of attitude formation towards trade. A large strand of informational effect is generated by political persuasion. Hicks et al. (2014) used district-level referendum results on Central America Free Trade Agreement (CAFTA) to prove that hypothesis. Left-leaning parties succeeded in having persuaded voters to oppose signing the FTA with the US. On the other hand, instead of political persuasion, some genuine policymaking can affect attitudes towards trade. According to "*embedded liberalism*" by Ruggie (1982), governmental policies shielding citizens from income shocks of

[1] https://rodrik.typepad.com/dani_rodriks_weblog/2008/06/stolper-samuelson-for-the-real-world.html.

trade liberalisation can result in higher support for free trade, which is confirmed by empirical findings concerning the positive influence of job-training programmes and welfare policies (Hays et al. 2005). It also seems that well-informed citizens, provided with facts about the assistance programmes are much more inclined to supportive attitudes towards trade.

Describing the influence of informational effect on attitudes towards free trade becomes complicated if the internet is considered. Framing and priming channels do not belong exclusively to the traditional media market anymore in most countries. The more complex the issue is (as free trade), the more tending people are to rely on the "*frames*" or "*leading narratives*" that help them to form the attitude, no matter how false a judgement lies behind it. Producing notable "*frames*" that easily reach social consciousness by simplifying or personalising the message is populists' *spécialité de la maison*. The so-called *elite cueing* might work as heuristics for individuals to lower the costs of forming an opinion on a specific FTA (Jungherr et al. 2018).

3.2 Economic Consensus: Interrupted Narrative

Economists, just like other social scientists, do not possess a magic wand or a crystal ball and therefore are doomed to make mistakes when making predictions and taking decisions under uncertainty. This probably has never been more evident than in the aftermath of the 2008 Great Recession when the chain of catastrophic economic events was blamed on the economists' inability to predict and prevent them. This attracted an unprecedented public outrage, anger, and crisis of confidence in the expertise of economists—a problem with which the discipline struggles to this day. This extremely powerful and severe crisis of trust experienced by economists is likely to have its roots in the occurrence and intensification of "*conflicts between symbolic powers that aim at imposing the vision of legitimate divisions*" (Bourdieu 1989, p. 22). According to Bourdieu, every "*symbolic power*" (i.e. one that has a vision and the power to change the world) rests on two pillars:

- "*symbolic capital*", which relates to the power to impose on others a vision of social divisions and depends on the social authority gained from previous skirmishes;
- "*symbolic efficacy*", which depends on the extent to which the proposed vision has real foundations.

Due to the particular dynamics of events and a certain conservatism of their attitudes, economists have lost a lot of both their "*symbolic capital*" and "*symbolic efficacy*".

From the mid-1970s for at least three decades, public opinion was dominated by the economists' view that the positive effects of international trade significantly outweighed its harmful impacts. When we look at Gregory Mankiw's (2006)[2] list of issues on which economists agreed based on surveys' results, we find that view of international trade on the high, second place. The statement that "*tariffs and import quotas usually reduce general economic welfare*" was consistently supported by 93% of the interviewed economists. When Dani Rodrik (2014)[3] characterised what the economic consensus was about, he said, "(...) *there are the errors of commission—cases in which economists' fixation on one particular model of the world makes them complicit in the administration of policies whose failure could have been predicted ahead of time. Economists' advocacy of neoliberal 'Washington Consensus' policies and financial globalisation falls into this category.*"

The evolution of economics as a social science favoured analytical approaches based on universalism.

> Mainstreameconomics became increasingly associated with abstractness and formalism, which went along with an ongoing trend that the history of economic theory was disregarded. (p. 76).
>
> The trade-off is that recent graduates of economic studies are more competent in the application of mathematics and statistics and ambitious computer simulations, than in having a working knowledge of the history of a specific subject. (p. 77).

One should also not forget about the very process of legitimising economists as experts in the public discourse. Fitzgerald and O'Rourke (2016) analysed economists' expert discourse based on three Irish economists' radio interviews. This analysis highlights two features of the economic discourse that the Authors consider to be particularly important for economic knowledge legitimacy. The first one, "*Judgment as Academic*", describes how economic experts refer to the need to listen to their expertise. The second one, "*Markets as Judgment*", argues that the markets' wisdom is deliberately brought to the fore as a kind of "*vis maior*". It strengthens the role of economists as experts, that is, those who, as a few and privileged due to the knowledge they possess, can correctly read this "*markets' judgment*".

[2] http://gregmankiw.blogspot.com/2006/11/consensus-of-economists.html.

[3] https://www.socialeurope.eu/perils-economic-consensus.

Maesse (2015, p. 279) links the sources of Bourdieu's "*symbolic power*" observed in economic expert discourses in the media to "*an elitism dispositif which emerged in the academic world of economics in the USA as an 'excellence myth*'". Among the factors legitimising economists as experts, one should also mention the Nobel Memorial Prize's symbolic role in Economic Sciences. Lebaron (2006) describes the role as the driving force behind the "*process of the social construction of public intellectuals*". Thus, economists become "*intellectual producers*" who can "*demonstrate their sphere of activity and legitimacy in order to take positions on various moral or political problems*". Of the various representatives of the social sciences, only economists are eligible to be nominated for the Nobel Prize. Perhaps this especially makes them prone to overconfidence?

In Colander (2005), we find empirical evidence of a sense of superiority among American economists perceiving themselves as leading representatives of social sciences—these are the results of research conducted in the form of survey and interviews with graduate students at seven top-ranking graduate economics programmes: University of Chicago, Columbia University, Harvard University, Massachusetts Institute of Technology, Stanford University, Yale University, and Princeton University. Seventy-seven per cent of the respondents believe in the economists' privileged position.

Fourcade et al. (2015) find out that the feeling of superiority may result from the formalisation of methods used by economists, which often justifies drawing far-reaching conclusions, as well as the high demand for their expert skills reflected in economists' high salaries and working for or with influential and wealthy clients. Fourcade et al. (2015, p. 91) also note: "*Economists' unique position gives them unusual power to accomplish changes in the world, it also exposes them more to conflicts of interests, critique, and mockery when things go wrong*".

Paul Krugman, a Nobel Prize winner and a formerly strong defender of globalisation, admits in his Bloomberg column (2019)[4] that "*during the 1990s, a number of economists (…) tried to figure out how much the changing trade landscape was contributing to rising inequality. They generally concluded that the effect was relatively modest and not the central factor in the widening income gap. So academic interest in the possible adverse effects of trade, while it never went away, waned.*" Krugman is ready to wear

[4] https://www.bloomberg.com/opinion/articles/2019-10-10/inequality-globalization-and-the-missteps-of-1990s-economics.

sackcloth and ashes, so many economists are (see, e.g., Catão and Obstfeld 2019), and they acknowledge that the impact of exports on jobs and inequality was strongly underestimated. What is right for the long run, might be wrong in the shorter perspective. Therefore, trade imbalances brought about rapid changes may result in transitionary adjustments and drops in employment, which might be concentrated in some industry sectors or geographical areas. Again, coming back to Krugman's argument (2019[5]), the US trade deficit surge "*reduced the share of manufacturing in GDP by around 1.5 percentage points, or more than 10%, which means that it explains more than half of the roughly 20% decline in manufacturing employment between 1997 and 2005*".

The outbreak of the GFC in 2008 interrupted the period of strong growth, low and stable inflation, and limited macroeconomic uncertainty previously observed in the world economy. With the onset of a recession, there was an immense social disenchantment with economists as experts. It was a pivotal moment in which an intense public discussion about neoliberalism was initiated. The previously known "*economic consensus*" developed over the decades lost its ground. The close relationship between international trade and prosperity burst with a wave of human emotions and anger, fuelled by the adverse effects of bankruptcies, job losses, and the impoverishment of local communities. Those changes provided a grim picture of the social consequences of globalisation, in which the impact of free trade on jobs no longer appeared rosy. A noticeable change took place in the trade and economic narratives observed in the public discourse. Intense criticism of the (neo)liberal model was coupled with a new narrative promoting a retreat from the free market's principles, of which many were seen as the root causes of the economic pain. However, as Birdsall and Fukuyama (2011, p. 45) note, the calls for a revision of the capitalist approach, which began to be clearly articulated with the onset of the global crisis, were not evenly voiced in terms of geopolitical interests:

> *No leader of a major developing country has backed away from his or her commitment to free trade or the global capitalist system. Instead, the established Western democracies are the ones that have highlighted the risks of relying too much on market-led globalisation and called for greater regulation of global finance.*

[5] Ibid.

Further, the authors symbolically recall the rather uncompromising words of the former Brazilian president Lula da Silva who expressed the following opinion in 2009:[6]

> *This crisis was fostered and boosted by irrational behavior of some people that are white, blue-eyed. Before the crisis they looked like they knew everything about economics, and they have demonstrated they know nothing about economics.*

Birdsall and Fukuyama (2011) emphasise that the previous experiences of crisis episodes that some Latin American and Asian countries went through, in particular in the 1990s, "*immunised them*" to the utterly uncritical adaptation of the ideas associated with the Washington consensus, particularly that of its strong reliance on foreign capital. Before the critical year of 2008, these countries had prudently accumulated high levels of foreign currency reserves and ensured an appropriate regulation and control level over the domestic banking sector. It is hard not to notice that countries outside the strict club of highly developed countries (whose members have dominated the world economy for decades) have historically always remained critical of economic liberalism for many reasons. Inter alia, one can indicate the distinctiveness of their own systems of values and cultural conditions, permanently in line with the inevitability of conflicts with the "West", reaching even the colonialism times.

The steadfastness and enormous consistency of positions presented under the "*economic consensus*", which served as a unanimous-sounding narrative before the GFC, do not apply equally to the whole world. The stamping of "*frames*" for the "*whole world*" in the public discourse was mostly shaped by the Western experts, fluent in expressing their thoughts in English, usually educated at the Western universities, often referring to the same scientific authorities and traditions. Moreover, they would typically come from countries ranked as rich and influential GVCs creators. Their "*symbolic power*" was, therefore, fully reflected in their "*symbolic efficacy*".

The eurozone crisis, which started spreading throughout the European Union in 2010, revealed significant differences between the member states regarding their own, culturally determined interpretations of the free-market economy's principles, their levels of competitiveness, and their

[6] https://www.theguardian.com/world/2009/mar*/26/lula-attacks-white-bankers-crash.

needs dictated by experiencing the crisis. For example, the CEE countries, especially Poland, despite the empirical evidence of their business cycles' synchronisation with "old Europe", weathered the crisis better than the old member states. Poland praised itself for being a "*green island*" and recording positive economic growth rates throughout the whole crisis. Quite a unique path of socio-economic transformation, from a centrally planned economy to a free-market economy, placed post-communist countries in the position of "*continuously catching-up contenders*". On the other hand, it also offered leverage, which means jumping over several levels of the development ladder at once, omitting less successful phases, and giving access and the possibility to implement solutions devoid of "*youth indiscretion*", which burdened the performance of "*their older colleagues*". Access to the EU structural funds, powerful injections of public investment, (initial) enthusiasm for the free-market models, a great drive to get established in the global economy created a completely different "*momentum*" in the CEE countries, both in terms of objectively defined macroeconomic achievements and social moods as well as popular emotional layers.

Among the old member states, the crisis's roots grew from the soil of the institutional asymmetry between the North and South's political economies. Northern European economies operated export-driven, long-run growth models, underpinning the monetary union's success. The Southern economies pursued other demand-driven growth models, which severely limited their effective long-term performance without the possibility of devaluation (Hall 2014). As it is well-known, the Greek departure from the eurozone was a seriously considered scenario; both as a variant of "*cutting off the debt burden*" by the EU and the direction desired by those Greeks who saw in the independent exchange rate regime an emergency exit to regain competitiveness and improve macroeconomic outcomes. However, the then Greek Minister of Finance, Yanis Varoufakis—and a bit later a political celebrity, author of widely read books in which he fiercely criticises the elite and capitalism—was extremely sceptical about *Grexit* in 2011, saying, "*The exit from the euro for a deficit country would send us back to the neolithic period before we could even realise it*".[7]

While the economic crisis in the Eurozone has further increased the divergence between the core and the southern periphery, at the same time,

[7] https://www.businessinsider.com/in-2011-greek-finance-minister-yanis-varoufakis-said-grexit-would-send-us-back-to-the-neolithic-age-2015-6?IR=T.

the cooperation between the German industry and the CEE region has strengthened, shifting important components of GVCs there. The expansion of the German industry supply network towards the East, coupled with continued constraints in domestic demand by the major euro area economies, has gone hand in hand with the impoverishment of Southern European regions' production matrix and, more generally, with a general diversion of trade flows.

In this way, elites and experts from the old member states experienced a kind of catharsis, gaining a more and more critical view of the economic consensus, which not by accident coincided with unfavourable macroeconomic conditions. At the same time, many of their colleagues from the new member states, overwhelmed by the "catch-up processes", tightened the neoliberal course. As Bugaric (2012, p. 3) writes:

> *Under the strong influence of the Washington consensus and its rule of law paradigm, they [CEE countries] developed a distinct type of developmental state, a neoliberal developmental state. Not an oxymoron, this type of developmental state is characterised by excessively formalised regulatory structures, a strong reliance on pro market (neoliberal) economic policies and an almost complete neglect of autonomous developmental policies.*

However, it must be admitted that the wide range of the post-crisis reflections that emerged did not stop the wave of populism[8] either in old or new EU member states. Populist leaders took over the political scene in Europe by storm ("take no prisoners").

3.3 "New Preachers on When Calls the Heart"

In 2014, Thomas Piketty entered the arena of the heated expert and public debate with his book *Capital in the Twenty-First Century*. According to The Economist (2014),[9] "*the book's success had a lot to do with being about the right subject at the right time. Inequality had suddenly become a fevered topic, especially in America. Having for years dismissed the gaps between the haves and have-nots as a European obsession, Americans, stung by the excesses of Wall Street, were suddenly talking about the rich and redistribution.*"

[8] "Cas Mudde has been influential in the literature, suggesting that populist philosophy is a loose set of ideas that share three core features: anti-establishment, authoritarianism, and nativism" (Inglehart and Norris 2016, p. 7).

[9] https://www.economist.com/leaders/2014/05/03/a-modern-marx.

Thomas Piketty seems to fit perfectly into the frontman's role, the horseman of the apocalypse, probably riding the symbolically white horse. It is worth noting that the meaning of personification—giving a specific idea a specific face in public discourse has been known for a very long time (since ancient Greece). Katz and Lazarsfeld (1955), in their oft-cited study "*Personal Choice*", laid the foundations for the understanding of what makes an "*influencer*". The authors describe the "*two-step flow of communication*" mechanism in which the impact of media content does not reach the audience directly but instead is passed by the intermediation of personal networks formed by specific people that communicate with each other. In this process, individuals are referred to as "*opinion leaders*". They interpret everyday life, as well as current events, to shape the opinions of others and manage the collective imagination.

Although Katz and Lazarsfeld's approach was superseded by the media effects theories, which considered traditional media to be the main actors of the public debate, the development of technology and social media not only brought influencers back into the fore but even put them on a high pedestal. The level of ferocity of attacks on Piketty by other expert economists (incredibly shortly after the publication of the book) can be considered a measure of the strength of the impact of the "*economic consensus*" and its importance for the formation of economic views. It is quite significant that, although since the outbreak of the GFC, the expert discourse among economists revealed more and more differences and a critical attitude towards "*mainstream, conventional economics*", the counter-arguments to Piketty's study were formulated mainly in the neoliberal spirit, as confirmed by the results of Rieder and Theine (2019) who studied British and Irish and Austrian and German responses to Piketty's publication. The authors support the hypothesis of "*'non-death' of mainstream economic thinking in public discourses*".

The election of Donald Trump as the president of the United States and the result of the 2016 Brexit referendum in the UK can be considered as other important events shaping the course of public discourse and the role of economic consensus. As Vine (2020) writes, the liberal media and academia reacted to these events "*with a frantic attempt to rationalise*". Vine's somewhat provocative sounding questions (2020, p. 467) seem to reflect well the direction of the transformations of expert discourse:

Why is it that we habitually invoke the works of Marx, Braverman and Foucault (for example), but typically ignore the contributions of Burke, Durkheim and

Hayek (again, for example)? Are we genuinely content to conflate critical scholarship with left-wing politics? Yes, we critical scholars are politically prejudiced. Through an intellectual echo chamber, we have fashioned a critical consensus.

Certainly, Trump fundamentally changed the way of political communication, as he wrote on his Twitter on 10 November 2012: "*Thanks—many are saying I'm the best 140 character writer in the world*". By legitimising Twitter as the official medium of communication, he facilitated the advent of a new standard of public debate to all and sundry—a debate in which emotions become its full participant, a debate in which no experts are needed, a debate in which there are no intermediaries between himself and his voters. During the Brexit campaign and the US presidential election, the elite (including scientists and experts) were the subject of numerous attacks. Smith et al. (2020) estimate that during the campaign preceding the Brexit referendum, the pro-Leave media (mainly tabloids) showed approval and support for anti-elite rhetoric in as much as 90% of the content they surveyed. Furthermore, the leading tone of Trump's election campaign was most clearly described by Wayne Robert LaPierre, a well-known American gun-rights activist and Trump supporter, who said[10]: "*the three most dangerous voices in America: academic elites, political elites, and media elites*".

Exaggeration, emotional rhetoric, and aggressiveness, so characteristic for the language of populists, are not conducive to honest reflection. When trying to get rid of these flashy and sinister labels and ask whether the criticism directed at expert elites had any in-depth justification, populists' diagnosis may be worth considering. Blok and Lemmens (2015) note that European research programmes dedicated to supporting responsible innovation can be criticised for being designed to quite dogmatically support economic growth and placing an excessive emphasis on the promotion of neoliberal values. More broadly, excessive and too one-sided succumbing to neoliberal values in organising, financing, and evaluating science, social sciences in particular, appear a frequently formulated accusation. As a consequence, it comes to "routinised knowledge-producing" instead of "knowledge-creation" (see Leino et al. 2018; Cheek 2017), to atomisation and individualisation of research activities instead of teamwork (Erkkilä and Piironen 2015), to displace the normative approach in

[10] https://www.latimes.com/politics/la-na-pol-trump-elites-20170725-story.html.

favour of positivism, as well as the corporatisation of higher education and precarious situation of (mostly early-stage) researchers (Cannella and Koro-Ljungberg 2017).

Trump's Twitter kingdom stretched relatively freely beyond virtual reality—his administration actively cheered on Brexit and undermined the European integration processes, questioned former US global security alliances, such as NATO, and openly supported economic nationalism by declaring its opposition to the post-war liberal international consensus. The philosophy of the nation-state's primacy and Trump's "*transactionism*" entailed real changes in trade policy. Trump attempted to play the role of a new demiurge who "*restores order, splendour, and dignity*". This populist narrative reveals the so far insufficient satisfaction of many people to be treated as little cogs in a big machine of the mainstream summed up by "*It's the economy, stupid*". In his exaggerated and propaganda-style of "making America great again", Trump paradoxically revealed many of the American weaknesses and showed the strength of other economies.

It is difficult to discuss the American economy without mentioning its connections to the rest of the world. Inevitably, trade interdependencies are at the heart of any American economic debate. Trump's narrative contains a lot of "*victimhood*", according to which the US is perpetually exploited, treated "*unfairly*", and the resulting trade imbalances are the measure of this unfair treatment. This surprising combination of preaching and business talk becomes a new, quite convincing, and ubiquitous narrative—a specific type of argumentation referring to a specific sense of morality, smoothly woven into the world of business logic. Examples of this "*new quality*" of the public debate include Trump's criticism of Germany's trade surplus with the US. In arguing that German imports are harming the American manufacturing industry, Trump made the following statements:[11] (1) "*The Germans are bad, very bad", (2) "See the millions of cars they sell in the US, terrible. We will stop this". (3) "If you want to build cars in the world, then I wish you all the best. You can build cars for the United States, but for every car that comes to the USA, you will pay 35 percent tax.*" This is how Trump builds his symbolic capital.

[11] https://finance.yahoo.com/news/trump-reportedly-calls-germans-very-081255668.html?guccounter=1&guce_referrer=aHR0cHM6Ly93d3cuZ29vZ2xlLmNvbS8&guce_referrer_sig=AQAAAA4WXN1ZCW_WNm5gKbBl2VOSp5_ODkUfC12iwmIxAVarc6QlhNcXKtdGVw37PgCQjGwSk8C9gkG6kxi78Ic_h6uRSN-r2nS9xZ3Q6bcg74uYLjMcji2HhDV0VooV5idN7IPzm8NhPVCmCmyT_XbVvKDjfQ_-nHlUWaA0L7H2BXK5f.

Trump's "*symbolic efficacy*" is rooted in reality. Germany along with China and the US make up the top three global exporters. China has been in the top three since 2013, threatening the US leadership position it has held for decades. The same three countries have been at the fore in the world of high-tech exports for a long time. In 2004 China outclassed the US as the leader in this ranking, and then in 2010 Germany (for the second time—the first time it happened in 2004) took the second place, pushing the American power to the third place. In 2017, Hong Kong pushed the United States out of the three and outclassed Germany as a high-tech exporter, taking second place.

National Security Advisor O'Brien presented the change in attitude towards China in the US foreign policy:[12]

> *For decades, Donald J. Trump was one of the few prominent Americans to recognise the true nature of the Chinese Communist Party and its threat to America's economic and political way of life. Now, under President Trump's leadership, the United States is taking action to protect our nation and its partners from an increasingly assertive China. We are no longer turning a blind eye to the People's Republic of China's conduct nor are we hiding our criticism of its Communist Party behind closed doors.*

Vice President Pence gave a clear interpretation of these assumptions:[13]

> *In our National Security Strategy that the President Trump released last December* [2017], *he described a new era of "great power competition". Foreign nations have begun to, as we wrote, "reassert their influence regionally and globally", and they are "contesting [America's] geopolitical advantages and trying [in essence] to change the international order in their favor". In this strategy, President Trump made clear that the United States of America has adopted a new approach to China. We seek a relationship grounded in fairness, reciprocity, and respect for sovereignty, and we have taken strong and swift action to achieve that goal.*

[12] "Trump On China. Putting America First. Collection of speeches laying out the most significant United States foreign policy shift in a generation", edited by Robert C. O'Brien, 2020, p. 1.

https://china.usc.edu/sites/default/files/article/attachments/trump-2020-Trump-on-China-Putting-America-First.pdf.

[13] Ibid., pp. 6–7.

Once again, we are dealing with an increasingly recognised phenomenon of the populist narrative, which causes cognitive dissonance. On the one hand, it contains exceptionally accurately diagnosed social problems, and on the other hand, it is destructive and polarising because of its exaggerated rhetoric and lack of well-thought-out solutions, thus unable to fit within intellectually permissible limits of expert discourse. The accuracy of the diagnoses underlying Trump's narrative, giving it a "*symbolic efficacy*", gained traction and attention. It forced a visible change in the expert narrative and the language used to express and communicate it.

Nevertheless, it was Thomas Piketty, a European (non-Anglophone) economist, who created a new substantive universe of debate and proposed a new language. It is difficult to ignore the exceptionality of the situation in which the catharsis of the American (Anglophone) experts must be set in motion externally. It can be true that the mainstream Anglophone experts are somehow in need of help to get out of their narrative bubble and to confront reality in a different way than the one which would be in line with the global economy rulers' perception. That state of confusion slightly reminds Gregor Samsa's state of mind. He is the protagonist of Kafka's "*Metamorphosis*" who says: "*I cannot make you understand. I cannot make anyone understand what is happening inside me. I cannot even explain it to myself.*"

3.4 A New Narrative? There Is Always an Angle

As Cook writes (2019, pp. 35–36):

> The floodgates of inequality economics have opened. (p. 35)
>
> The "Piketty Effect" has spread into political and policymaking circles as well. (p. 36).

Additionally, the COVID-19 pandemic has enhanced the voice of those who see protectionism as a trade policy-effective instrument.

A random review of the recent book titles devoted to "*trade wars*", and sold on Amazon, instinctively evokes associations with a new ("Piketty'ed") economic narrative. It is worth noting that the titles presented in Table 3.1 include works published after 2016, that is in the period marked by the Trump presidency and the Brexit referendum. Books were searched in Amazon's Business & Money Department based on their subject matter's relevance to the keyword "trade wars". The top seller—appealing to Karl Marx's legacy—suggests that readers should treat trade wars as class wars.

In Table 3.2, the marketing description of the same book on Amazon contains even more references to Marx's vocabulary, such as: "*interests of*

Table 3.1 List of works on "trade wars" published after 2016

Keyword	*Source*	*Sort by*	*Already published between 2016 and 2020 as on 27 November 2020*
Trade war	*Amazon/Books/ Money& Business Dept.*	*"Featured"*	

Titles	*Publishing year*
1. Trade Wars Are **Class Wars**: How Rising Inequality Distorts the Global Economy and Threatens International Peace	2020
2. The United States-China Trade War: Conflict Between the World's Economic Superpowers	2019
3. Trade War: Containers Don't Lie, Navigating the Bluster	2020
4. US Vs China: From Trade War To Reciprocal Deal	2019
5. Sinews of War and Trade: Shipping and **Capitalism** in the Arabian Peninsula	2020
6. Trade Wars on E Street: The ITC in the 1980s	2019
7. Stealth War: How China Took Over While America's **Elite** Slept	2019
8. Why Globalization Works for America: How Nationalist Trade Policies Are Destroying Our Country	2020
9. Superpower Showdown: How the Battle Between Trump and Xi Threatens a New Cold War	2020
10. The **New Class War**: Saving Democracy from the Managerial **Elite**	2020

elites", "*at the expense of workers*", and "*rising inequality*". The list of the ten most relevant search results includes more references to "*elite*", "*class struggle*", and, somewhat pejoratively used, "*capitalism*". Some of those books' marketing descriptions cleverly oscillate between the non-aligned objective sound of expert rationality, and the emotionality taken almost directly from street mass protests. Sometimes it is difficult to understand whether the authors identify with a particular type of "*populist sensitivity*" or formulate a critical judgement.

In response to the populist narrative, the expert narrative leaned towards left-wing sensitivity, became somewhat emotional, and invoked ethical and moral aspects. The latter seems to create new foundations for the universalism of the proclaimed views so that the new expert narrative could be easily disseminated. The narrative refers to the old film noir genre, somehow. There is a simple division into good guys and bad guys. There is always one good lonesome cowboy at the end of the film, one

Table 3.2 Marketing descriptions of books on trade wars presented on Amazon

Title	*Book description on Amazon*
Trade Wars Are Class Wars: How Rising Inequality Distorts the Global Economy and Threatens International Peace	A provocative look at how today's trade conflicts are caused by governments promoting **the interests of elites** at the expense of workers "This is a very important book."—Martin Wolf, *Financial Times* "The authors weave a complex tapestry of monetary, fiscal and social policies through history and offer opinions about what went right and what went wrong. … Worth reading for their insights into the history of trade and finance."—George Melloan, *Wall Street Journal* Longlisted for the 2020 Financial Times & McKinsey Business Book of the Year Award and named a Best Business Book of 2020 by Strategy + Business. Trade disputes are usually understood as conflicts between countries with competing national interests, but as Matthew C. Klein and Michael Pettis show, they are often the unexpected result of domestic political choices **to serve the interests of the rich at the expense of workers and ordinary retirees**. Klein and Pettis trace the origins of today's trade wars to decisions made by politicians and business leaders in China, Europe, and the United States over the past thirty years. Across the world**, the rich have prospered while workers can no longer afford to buy what they produce**, have lost their jobs, or have been forced into higher levels of debt. In this thought-provoking challenge to mainstream views, the authors provide a cohesive narrative that shows how **the class wars** of **rising inequality** are a threat to the global economy and international peace—and what we can do about it.
Sinews of War and Trade: Shipping and Capitalism in the Arabian Peninsula	A wide-ranging account of shipping and capitalism in the Middle East. On the map of global trade, China is now the factory of the world. A parade of ships full of raw commodities—iron ore, coal, oil—arrive in its ports, and fleets of container ships leave with manufactured goods in all directions. The oil that fuels China's manufacturing comes primarily from the Arabian Peninsula. Much of the material shipped from China are transported through the ports of Arabian Peninsula, Dubai's Jabal Ali port foremost among them. China's "maritime silk road" flanks the Peninsula on all sides. Sinews of War and Trade is the story of what the making of new ports and shipping infrastructures has meant not only for the Arabian Peninsula itself, but for the region and the world beyond. The book is the account of how maritime transportation is not simply an enabling adjunct of trade, but **central to the very fabric of global capitalism**. The ports that serve maritime trade, logistics, and hydrocarbon transport create racialised hierarchies of labour, engineer the lived environment**, aid the accumulation of capital regionally and globally, and carry forward colonial regimes of profit, law and administration**.

Trade Wars on E Street: The ITC in the 1980s	Alfred Eckes, a former chairman and commissioner of the US International Trade Commission, offers an inside look at trade administration during the 1980s. During that difficult decade, hundreds of American firms sought relief from surging and unfairly traded imports. The book, based on his personal diaries, shows how a bipartisan group of commissioners battled an uncompromising protectionist and rigid deregulators. They sought to undermine the trade remedy process, carefully crafted by Congress and the Executive to implement America's international agreements, and to **assure a fair hearing for industries and workers claiming import-related injury.**
The New Class War: Saving Democracy from the Managerial Elite	In both Europe and North America, populist movements have shattered existing party systems and thrown governments into turmoil. The embattled establishment claims that these populist insurgencies seek to overthrow liberal democracy. The truth is no less alarming but is more complex: Western democracies are being torn apart by a **new class war**. In this controversial and groundbreaking new analysis, Michael Lind, one of America's leading thinkers, debunks the idea that the insurgencies are primarily the result of bigotry, traces how the breakdown of mid-century class compromises between business and labor led to the conflict, and reveals the real battle lines. On one side is the **managerial overclass**—the university-credentialed elite that clusters in high-income hubs and dominates government, the economy and the culture. On the other side is the **working class** of the low-density heartlands—mostly, but not exclusively, native and white. The two classes clash over immigration, trade, the environment, and social values, and the managerial class has had the upper hand. As a result of the half-century decline of the institutions that once empowered the **working class**, power has shifted to the institutions the overclass controls: corporations, executive and judicial branches, universities, and the media. The **class war** can resolve in one of three ways: • The triumph of the **overclass**, resulting in a high-tech caste system. • The empowerment of populist, resulting in no constructive reforms. • A class compromise that provides **the working class with real power.** Lind argues that Western democracies must incorporate working-class majorities of all races, ethnicities, and creeds into decision making in politics, the economy, and culture. Only this class compromise can avert a never-ending cycle of clashes between **oligarchs** and populists and save democracy.

hero that saves the world in a white hat and riding a white horse. Consequently, there is a well-defined Schwarzcharacter, too, to be blamed for everything and then punished.

Klein and Pettis (2020) chase such Schwarzcharacter and succeed while writing admittedly: "*there is a problem with rich people*". To be more specific, among those "*rich people*", "*Euroglut*" is primarily worth stigmatising, that is, the restrained Germans and others (undefined) Europeans who, by suppressing domestic demand and limiting public spending, increase poverty. The Germans make their workers pay for the trade surplus reducing wages and working hours to influence German competitiveness through the capital to labour ratio. Cathy Feingold, Director of the International Department of America's Unions, refines this narrative in a debate inspired by Klein and Pettis (2020). She says:[14]

> *We need to change the objectives of trade. (…) This is not about if you are a protectionist or free trader but what are the objectives of the trade policy, and do these trade policies benefit working people. They can be part of the global economy and live lives with dignity. (…) You need workers rights in the multilateral trading system.*

These certainly accurate postulates, however, leave much understatement. Why have the workers' rights never before been so often the subject of mainstream Anglophone public debate in the context of the initial stage of outsourcing and offshoring decisions? Why is the topic of labour rights warming up precisely at the time when the United States is losing its competitive position in the world, the US trade deficit with China is growing year by year, and the estimated job loss in the period 2001–2018 is 3.7 million, including the loss of these jobs in manufacturing amounts to 2.8 million, taking account of 1.4 jobs lost in the production of electronic and computer parts? Does concern for workers' rights indeed apply equally to workers from developing and emerging countries who have gained higher income levels often thanks to their inclusion in global supply chains (GVCs)?

Undoubtedly the emerging economies play a significant and diverse role in GVCs nowadays. Their participation in GVCs has helped them create jobs and raise wages (WTO 2019). The increase in employment and wages was achieved in the exporting sector and indirectly through the links between exporting companies and other domestic companies.

[14] https://www.youtube.com/watch?v=_8WOSt41PSg.

Demand for workers related to the expansion of GVCs in developing countries is skill-biased. GVCs enable technology transfer and dissemination of innovation, which has a substantial impact on the labour market. Potential threats to the development of labour markets in developing countries may include the excess of unskilled labour and too much involvement of these countries in such GVCs segments that require lower qualifications. However, it seems that these negative trends may, to some extent, be counteracted by increasing labour demand fuelled by domestic consumption boost in large emerging economies such as China and India. In Europe, as a result of the effective inclusion of the CEE countries in GVCs, a change of the core-periphery division is taking place, affecting the labour market performance in these countries. The CEE economies are characterised by a significantly larger dependence on GVCs, as opposed to Southern and North-Western Europe (Grodzicki and Geodecki 2016).

The positive elements of the assessment of the impact of GVC integration on the labour markets in catching-up countries must not weaken the message of the need to enforce workers' rights across all countries of the world economy, that is respecting the rights to benefits, rights to association, and normalising working conditions. Nevertheless, a full assessment of the effects of the current situation on workers in the global economy covers a broader field of issues than just class or trade wars.

There are other ramifications for the active presence of developing and emerging countries in GVCs. The new "breed" of GVCs is led by MNEs from large, emerging economies (especially China and India) and combines operational efficiency with societal goals defined by the political system of the home country. Hence, political actors exercise considerable influence over GVC configuration (Kano et al. 2020).

The emergence of a new quality of business leadership combined with new centres of political power and a new, culturally distant (for the Western leaders) model of operations also creates entirely new conditions for the "*symbolic efficacy*". Experts from the circles of current leaders, however, being human beings with their emotions, preferences, likes, and identity, may show a natural tendency to succumb to the desire to maintain their narrative ("*symbolic capital*"), to keep it alive and strong, and to restore its "*symbolic power*".

3.5 Summarising Remarks

The economic consensus as a leading narrative belonging to the "*white, blue-eyed people*", as characterised by Brazil's President Lula da Silva, seems to be expiring. It used to provide a stable background for disputes over the direction of the trade policy, but it has itself come under strain. Eventually, trade effects turned out to be much more diversified and less optimistic than it was originally expected. The prevalence of the trade narrative based on the economic consensus fuelled the bulk of the world's public opinion for a substantial time. That corresponds to the US leadership in many aspects, both "symbolic power" and "symbolic efficacy" of the narrative derived from America's sphere of influence.

It is difficult to say whether, in the era of such a large heterogeneity of media, one can expect a new, equally coherent, and universally acceptable narrative. However, we live in a world of tense relations between the West and the East, in which China is fighting for the position of a world leader. Trade wars are tangible proof that the current order in the global economy is subject to significant changes. Narratives are an important weapon in this war and all other geopolitical "battlefronts", as they legitimise its purposefulness.

The observed left-turn in the media coverage and literature on trade is, on the one hand, a result of the well-placed diagnosis of reality. Without a doubt, we are dealing with income inequalities and social exclusions that require new awareness and new policy. On the other hand, this sensitivity is awakening among English-speaking public opinion makers quite late, even though these problems have existed for a long time in many places worldwide.

For example, why social issues and working conditions did not receive a greater amount of attention and scrutiny at the very beginning of the offshoring processes? The Havana Charter of 1947 ("Final Act of the United Nations Conference on Trade and Employment") set as one of its main objectives "*to facilitate the solution of problems relating to international trade in the fields of employment, economic development, commercial policy, business practices and commodity policy*". Moreover, the fundamental principle of its Chapter II was that "*full and productive employment is not a matter solely of domestic concern to a country but affects the economic wellbeing of all other countries. So, while domestic measures must be the prime means of avoiding unemployment, there must also be concerted international action to this end, under the sponsorship of the Economic and Social Council in collaboration with the appropriate intergovernmental agencies.*" Hopefully, more than seven decades later, these assumptions will get the attention of key decision-makers enough to be put into practice. This is to be believed, even if it may be the swan song of a collapsing empire ("*The king is dead, long live the king!*") rather than true sensitivity to social problems behind the new narrative.

References

Birdsall, N., & Fukuyama, F. (2011). The Post-Washington consensus: Development after the crisis. Foreign Affairs, 45–53.

Blok, V., & Lemmens, P. (2015). The emerging concept of responsible innovation. Three reasons why it is questionable and calls for a radical transformation of the concept of innovation. In Responsible innovation 2 (pp. 19–35). Cham: Springer.

Bögenhold, D. (2020). History of economic thought as an analytic tool: Why past intellectual ideas must be acknowledged as lighthouses for the future. International Advances in Economic Research, 26, 1–15.

Bourdieu, P. (1979). Symbolic power. Critique of Anthropology, 4(13–14), 77–85.

Bourdieu, P. (1989). Social space and symbolic power. Sociological Theory, 7(1), 14–25.

Bugaric, B. (2012). Law and Development in Central and Eastern Europe: Neoliberal Developmental State and Its Problems. Available at SSRN 2163073.

Cannella, G. S., & Koro-Ljungberg, M. (2017). Neoliberalism in higher education: Can we understand? Can we resist and survive? Can we become without neoliberalism?. Cultural Studies↔ Critical Methodologies, 17(3), 155–162.

Catão, L. & Obstfeld, M. (2019). Meeting Globalization's Challenges. Princeton: Princeton University Press. https://doi.org/10.1515/9780691198866

Cheek, N. N. (2017). Scholarly merit in a global context: The nation gap in psychological science. Perspectives on Psychological Science, 12(6), 1133–1137.

Cook, E. (2019). Historicizing Piketty: The Fall and Rise of Inequality Economics. In Histories of Global Inequality (pp. 35–57). Palgrave Macmillan, Cham.

Colander, D. (2005). The making of an economist redux. Journal of Economic Perspectives, 19(1), 175–198.

Colantone, I., & Stanig, P. (2018). Global competition and Brexit. American Political Science Review, 112(2), 201–218.

Dippel, C., Gold, R., & Heblich, S. (2016). Globalisation and anti-globalisation voters: Evidence from Germany. VOX: CEPR's Policy Portal, 10(7), 2016.

Dluhosch, B. (2018). Trade, inequality, and subjective well-being: Getting at the roots of the backlash against globalization (No. 741). LIS Working Paper Series.

Erkkilä, T., & Piironen, O. (2015). Autonomisation and individualisation: Ideational shifts in European higher education. Academic identities in higher education: The changing European landscape, 47–62.

Fitzgerald, J. K., & O'Rourke, B. K. (2016). Legitimising expertise: Analysing the legitimation strategies used by economics experts in broadcast interviews. Journal of Multicultural Discourses, 11(3), 269–282.

Fourcade, M., Ollion, E., & Algan, Y. (2015). The superiority of economists. Journal of Economic Perspectives, 29(1), 89–114.

Gawrońska-Nowak, B. (2019). Is Homo Oeconomicus an Extinct Species, and Does It Matter for EUropean Integration? Attitudes Towards Free Trade and Populism. *Global Discourse: An Interdisciplinary Journal of Current Affairs*, 9(1), 249–264.

Grodzicki, M. J., & Geodecki, T. (2016). New dimensions of core-periphery relations in an economically integrated Europe: The role of global value chains. Eastern European Economics, 54(5), 377–404.

Hall, P. A. (2014). Varieties of capitalism and the Euro crisis. West European Politics, 37(6), 1223–1243.

Hays, J. C., Ehrlich, S. D., & Peinhardt, C. (2005). Government spending and public support for trade in the OECD: An empirical test of the embedded liberalism thesis. International Organization, 59(2), 473–494.

Hicks, R., Milner, H. V., & Tingley, D. (2014). Trade policy, economic interests, and party politics in a developing country: The political economy of CAFTA-DR. International Studies Quarterly, 58(1), 106–117.

Inglehart, R. F., & Norris, P. (2016). *Trump, Brexit, and the Rise of Populism: Economic Have-Nots and Cultural Backlash* (No. RWP16-026). https://research.hks.harvard.edu/publications/workingpapers/Index.aspx.

Jungherr, A., Mader, M., Schoen, H., & Wuttke, A. (2018). Context-driven attitude formation: The difference between supporting free trade in the abstract and supporting specific trade agreements. Review of International Political Economy, 25(2), 215–242.

Kano, L., Tsang, E. W., & Yeung, H. W. C. (2020). Global value chains: A review of the multi-disciplinary literature. Journal of International Business Studies, 51, 577–622.

Katz, Elihu, & Lazarsfeld, Paul F. (1955). Personal influence. The part played by people in the flow of mass communication. New York: Free Press.

Klein, M. C., & Pettis, M. (2020). Trade wars are class wars: How rising inequality distorts the global economy and threatens international peace. Yale University Press.

Krugman, P. (2019, November). 6. Globalization: What Did We Miss?. In Meeting Globalization's Challenges (pp. 113–120). Princeton University Press.

Lebaron, F. (2006). "Nobel" economists as public intellectuals: The circulation of symbolic capital. International Journal of Contemporary Sociology, 43(1), 88–101.

Leino, H., Santaoja, M., & Laine, M. (2018). Researchers as knowledge brokers: Translating knowledge or co-producing legitimacy? An urban infill case from Finland. International Planning Studies, 23(2), 119–129.

Los, B., McCann, P., Springford, J., & Thissen, M. (2017). The mismatch between local voting and the local economic consequences of Brexit. Regional Studies, 51(5), 786–799.

Lü, X., Scheve, K., & Slaughter, M. J. (2012). Inequity aversion and the international distribution of trade protection. American Journal of Political Science, 56(3), 638–654.

Maesse, J. (2015). Economic experts: A discursive political economy of economics. Journal of Multicultural Discourses, 10(3), 279–305.

Mankiw, N. G. (2006). Reflections on the trade deficit and fiscal policy. Journal of Policy Modeling, 28(6), 679–682.

Mansfield, E. D., & Mutz, D. C. (2009). Support for free trade: Self-interest, sociotropic politics, and out-group anxiety. International Organization, 63(3), 425–457.

Mutz, D. C., & Kim, E. (2017). The impact of in-group favoritism on trade preferences. International Organization, 71(4), 827–850.

Piketty, Thomas (2014). Capital in the twenty-first century. Cambridge: The Belknap Press of Harvard University Press.

Rieder, M., & Theine, H. (2019). 'Piketty is a genius, but...': An analysis of journalistic delegitimation of Thomas Piketty's economic policy proposals. Critical Discourse Studies, 16(3), 248–263.

Rodrik, D. (2014). https://socialeurope.eu/perils-economic-consensus

Rodrik, D. (2018). https://rodrik.typepad.com/dani_rodriks_weblog/2008/06/stolper-samuelson-for-the-real-world.html

Ruggie, J. G. (1982). International regimes, transactions, and change: Embedded liberalism in the postwar economic order. International Organization, 36(2), 379–415.

Smith, D., Deacon, D., & Downey, J. (2020). Inside out: The UK press, Brexit and strategic populist ventriloquism. European Journal of Communication, 36, 0267323120940917.

Vine, T. (2020). Brexit, Trumpism and paradox: Epistemological lessons for the critical consensus. Organization, 27(3), 466–482.

WTO Annual Report. (2019) https://www.wto.org/english/res_e/publications_e/anrep19_e.htm

CHAPTER 4

Globalisation and International Trade in the Eyes of the Polish Society

Abstract The chapter compares the Polish society to its international peers to determine the extent to which FTA attitudes are country-specific, and to what extent they fit and connect with the pan-European perspectives. We look closer at the values relevant from the perspective of international trade and the processes of globalisation. How similar or how different are the Poles from other Central-Europeans? How specific is the perspective of transition countries compared to the states with established democracy? Prior to presenting the analyses that could get us closer to these answers, we are pointing to the consequences of the 2008 financial crisis noted and analysed by many sociologists. Especially interesting for us are the conclusions of Alain Touraine and Mirosława Marody. Then we analyse the results of international social surveys and find that the Polish society quite widely shares the image of living on the "underdeveloped" side of Europe and agrees that Poland is still "catching up" with the world's more successful parts. This comes together with quite a high level of legitimisation of income inequalities that suggests that Poles are generally quite optimistic about their chances to finally succeed in this "catching-up" process and believe it is possible to do by individual effort.

Keywords Attitudes towards trade • Values • Economic liberalism • Attitudes towards globalisation

B. Gawrońska-Nowak et al., *Trade Wins or Trade Wars*,
https://doi.org/10.1007/978-3-030-76997-0_4

In this chapter we look closer at the Polish society and its values relevant from the perspective of international trade and the processes of globalisation. How similar or how different are the Poles from other Central-Europeans? How specific is the perspective of transition countries compared to the states with established democracy? Prior to presenting the analyses that could get us closer to these answers, we are pointing to the consequences of the 2008 financial crisis and the ensuing Great Recession that has left its irreversible marks in all the developed societies, including the Polish.

Alain Touraine, a French sociologist, in his diagnosis of Western societies after the crisis of 2008, drew attention to several phenomena important from the point of view of the reality described in this chapter and this book. These are:

- Changes in the occupational structure of the population, in which the sphere of services is strongly dominant, and the sphere of production is transferred to poorer and less developed countries and regions.
- Growing social inequalities that substantially weaken the middle class and a change in the main axis of social conflicts, that is conflicts of interest that could be resolved within parliamentary democracies, are gradually replaced by conflicts related to cultural differences referring to different social identities.

All these, according to Touraine, mark the end of the "social world" and we can no longer describe actors by their place within social relationships (Touraine 2014, p. 111). Human beings as social actors are "*no longer motivated by their social and economic interests but instead by their desire to defend their rights*" (p. 112). We are witnessing the process of redefining actors from social to moral ones, defined by reference to the sets of values they recognise. An economy operating at the global level becomes detached from institutions and generally from forms of social organisation. For the first time in history, the world of production, banking, and technology is not connected to the actors' world, so the institutional and ideological (axiological) orders are not complementary. These phenomena foreshadow a profound civilisational change, and in the new organisation of society, the identities and values are going to play a leading role.

Mirosława Marody (2017, p. 51) distinguishes three types of "communities of meaning" formed around values and gaining importance in contemporary societies. The first one refers to the idea of economic success achieved through competition encompassing all spheres of life: the actions of individuals, companies, political parties, and states. The basic rules for the competition are provided by the idealised model of the free market. The overriding principle is to maximise profit and minimise losses.

The second type of community of meanings arises around a sense of community itself and basic social identities: religious, ethnic, territorial, national, or otherwise. The main principle that keeps together such a community is the defence against strangers. The criteria for being a stranger are established in the course of social practices. This type of communities questions the foundations of the existing systemic institutions and—or maybe even first of all—fights for a "common cause", which becomes the basis for shaping social identity. The cause can be environmental protection, a change in the law on abortion, a moral renewal of society, or something else.

The third type of communities distinguished by Marody is based on the desire to "be oneself". That is, to live in a manner consistent with one's preferences and opportunities created by reality. The primary justification for the existence of this community of meanings is the idea of self-realisation, and the recognition of the freedom of others to make choices other than our own, at least as long as they do not interfere with our freedom. Marody points out that this type of community is firmly embedded in a specific type of communication that emerged thanks to the development of the internet and social media.

The above described "communities of meanings" can be separated at the analytical level, but—as Marody points out—in practice, most citizens operate under the simultaneous influence of all three of them, so they come out in various social situations with different intensity. Most people act as they would like to "have their cake and eat it", that is, be economically successful and live in harmony with themselves while being part of a community fighting for the "cause" important to them. That is why the existence of these three communities of meaning does not necessarily translate to the particular types of non-social actors emerging around the described sets of values and does not establish institutions.

In the context of these processes that are currently observed in Western societies, we will analyse the Polish society that for a long period stayed aside of the mainstream of social and economic development being a communist country—a part of a parallel world.

Because of that historical experience, the very idea of transformation used to be such a "common cause" uniting a large part of the Polish society: building democracy or "catching up with Europe" gave meaning to institutions and set directions for social actors. Today, in the second decade of the twenty-first century, these ideas are gradually losing their importance partially because the transformation goals have been achieved (e. g. Poland's joined the European Union in 2004) and partially because the growing complexity of contemporary societies and economies is really hard to be imagined and described as the one linear process.

However, one should bear in mind that Poles entered the period of transformation with a quite idealised image of capitalism. This "facilitated (...) acceptance of the basic principles and values of a liberal economy" (Marody 2019) and resulted in quite a specific set of attitudes and beliefs regarding the economic development of the country. In contrast to the previous centrally planned one, the market economy and accession to the European Union, in contrast to the previous dominance of the Soviet Union, have become important signs of Poland's socio-economic transition and as such were practically not questioned.

4.1 Is Liberalism "Right" or "Left" in Poland?

In 2017, nearly 30 years since the beginning of transformation, the vast majority of Poles (78%)[1] still thought that economic growth was the country's highest priority. This percentage is high compared to the attitudes expressed by Poland's direct neighbours EU members: Slovakia (69%), Czech Republic (67%), and Germany (56%). Only in Lithuania, the number was higher (84%). When asked to choose between economic growth and environmental protection,[2] Poles were one of few European societies that stood on the side of the former. Among the surveyed EU members, only Lithuanians appeared to be more strongly convinced than Poles that

[1] The data quoted here and later in this chapter and referred to as EVS (European Values Study), were collected as a part of this international research project (www.europeanvaluesstudy.eu). In Poland the EVS survey was conducted at the end of 2017 and was financed by a grant from National Science Centre (Poland). Project no. 2016/21//B/HS6/03199.

[2] The question wording was the following: *Here are two statements people sometimes make when discussing the environment and economic growth. Which of them comes closer to your own point of view? (1) Protecting the environment should be given priority, even if it causes slower economic growth and some loss of jobs. (2) Economic growth and creating jobs should be the top priority, even if the environment suffers to some extent.*

economic growth is more important than environment protection (Fig. 4.1).

"Net preference" was calculated as the difference between the share of respondents preferring economic growth and those choosing environment protection. A negative value means that the latter percentage is greater than the former.

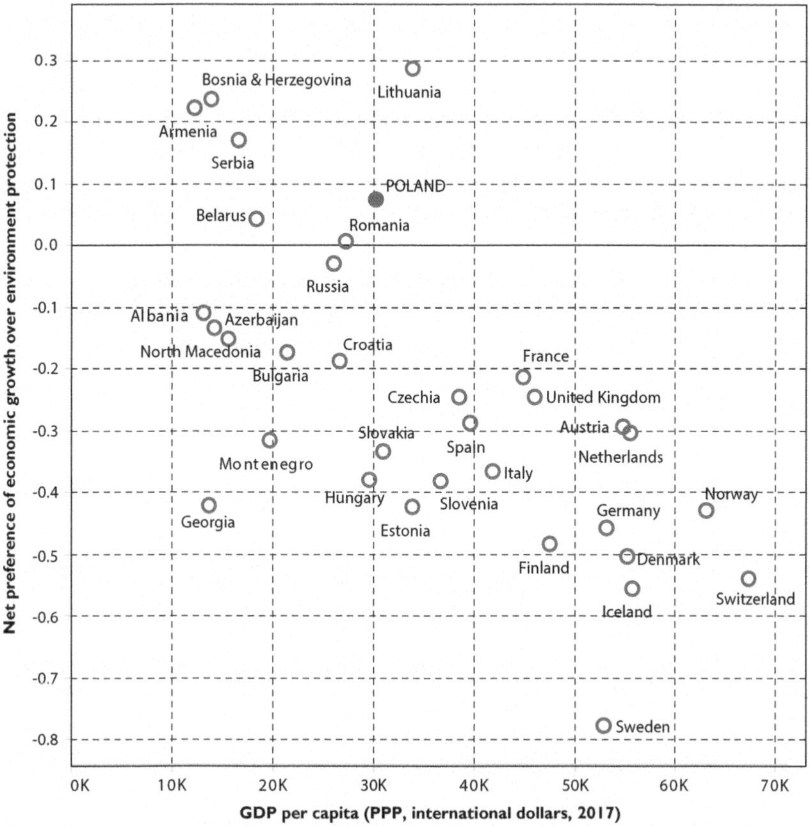

Fig. 4.1 Relationship between prioritising economic growth over environment protection and economic development (measured by GDP per capita). The figure presents all the countries that participated in the EVS survey. Correlation on country level is $r = -0.66$. (Data sources: EVS 2017 (own, calculations); GDP per capita—World Bank database)

The European Values Survey also shows that Poles still tend to accept basic principles of economic liberalism, such as private ownership of businesses, competition, or individual responsibility for meeting basic needs (Table 4.1). These attitudes remain to a great extent stable over the last 25 years (see Marody 2019, p. 60).

Part of this liberal (in the economic sense) attitude is also a widespread tendency to legitimise income inequalities, which is again more frequent among Poles than in their neighbours from the EU, and quite stable throughout the transformation. As one can see in Table 4.1, in 2017, 72% thought that income should reward individual effort and only 14% opted for making incomes more equal. In comparison, only 25% of respondents in Slovakia appeared to accept income inequalities, in Lithuania the figure stood at 26%, in the Czech Republic 34%, and in Germany 39%. The actual income inequalities measured by Eurostat are the lowest in Slovakia and the Czech Republic, where the acceptance of such inequalities was also the lowest.[3]

On the basis of EVS questions related to economic issues, we created the index of economic liberalism that counted the number of statements expressing the liberal views accepted by respondents (*competition is good*,

Table 4.1 Support for basic principles of liberalism (in %)

	1[a]	*2*	*3*	*4*	*5*	
Individuals should take more responsibility for providing for themselves	**15**	**17**	39	17	12	*The state should take more responsibility to ensure that everybody is provided for*
Competition is good	**43**	**21**	21	8	7	*Competition is harmful*
Incomes should be made more equal	9	5	14	**36**	**36**	*There should be greater incentives for individual effort*
Private ownership of business and industry should be increased	**13**	**14**	33	17	23	*Government ownership of business and industry should be increased*

Data source: EVS 2017, calculations by the author

[a]The scale was initially 1–10, as in the EVS questionnaire, but it has been recoded for greater clarity: 1 or 2 = 1; 3 or 4 = 2; 5 or 6 = 3; 7 or 8 = 4 and 9 or 10 = 5. The highlighted percentages are those in support of "economically liberal" position

[3] Eurostat measures the inequalities as income quintile share ratio. In 2018 it was 4.25 for Poland, 3.3 for Czech Republic, 3.5 for Slovakia (data from 2017), and 5.07 for Germany. Some Polish commentators question the accuracy of data on inequalities in Poland claiming they are more similar to the ones in the US than to Germany.

income should serve as an incentive for individual effort, ***private ownership of businesses should be increased***, and ***individuals should take more responsibility for providing for themselves***). The index took values from zero—when none of these statements was accepted, to four—when all of them were. From this index's perspective, Poland had the fifth highest mean value among 33 countries that participated in the EVS (Fig. 4.2).

It is not easy to explain such adherence of the Polish society to the principles of economic liberalism, especially when taking into account that Eurostat categorised about 15% of the population as "at risk of poverty"[4] and this rate was higher than in Poland's neighbours—EU members. One possible argument can refer to the characteristics of cultures proposed in the 1980s by Geert Hofstede, according to which Poles represent an individualistic culture (see the new edition: Hofstede et al. 2010). As Domański and Dukaczewska noticed (1995, p. 390), "the Polish individualism now (...) involves competitive striving to attain economic goals and occupational carrier". The statement was formulated a long time ago, at the beginning of Polish transformation, but the cited results of EVS survey suggest that this observation may still be valid. Another argument would refer to the low level of trust in the institutions of the Polish government.[5]

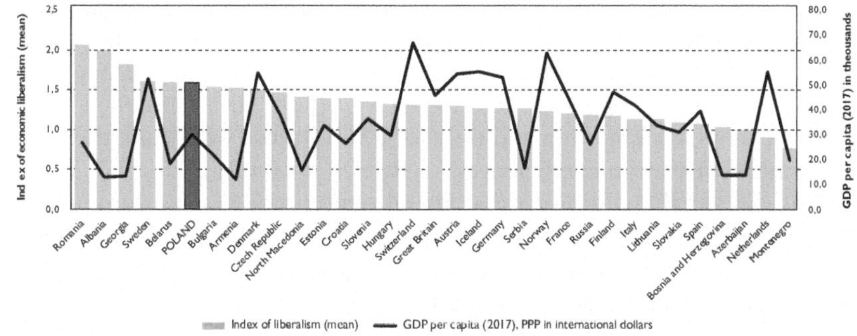

Fig. 4.2 Level of economic liberalism in 33 countries in 2017. Country-level correlation between index of liberalism and GDP per capita is r = -0.21. (Data sources: EVS 2017, own calculations; GDP per capita—from World Bank database)

[4] Below the income threshold of 60% of median equivalised income after social transfers.

[5] Net trust in Government and Parliament was negative in 2017 (-52 and -58 respectively), only the Army enjoyed quite a substantial positive net trust (42%). Net trust in police was also positive, but lower: 20%. Among distrusted institutions (with negative net trust) were also civil servants, social security system, system of justice, and political parties.

The state is usually given more say in delegitimising economic inequalities and questioning the market economy. Poland's net confidence (the difference between the percentages of trusting and not trusting) in all such state institutions as the Government, Parliament, the justice system, and social security system is negative. This, however, seems characteristic for the countries that started their transition to democracy after the collapse of the Eastern Bloc. In Western Europe at least the latter two enjoy a positive balance of confidence.

The in-depth analysis of economic liberalism of Poles shows that this attitude is not strongly related to the individual's situation, for example on a job market but it does correlate with his/her place in the social structure—the level of income ($r = 0.219$; $p < 0.001$)[6] and education ($r = 0.212$; $p < 0.001$). Attitudes towards economic freedom are also related to respondents' axiological orientation: those who are liberal in the economic sense tend to be liberal in a moral sense[7] as well ($r = 0.199$, $p < 0.001$) and distrust the Catholic Church ($r = 0.172$, $p < 0.001$).

Due to this interrelation of both senses of liberalism—moral and economic—Poles demonstrate a paradoxical understanding of left and right political views (see also Wojcik et al. 2019). Self-positioning on a left-right scale depends on moral liberalism ($r = -0.428$, $p < 0.001$), although economic views affect it as well, even if their influence is weaker. Economic liberalism is rather a part of left-wing than right-wing political orientation ($r = -0.078$, $p < 0.02$). "Eliminating big inequalities in income between citizens" is a very important goal for 41% of those who self-define their political views as right-wing and only for 25% of those who think they are left-wing. Correlation coefficient is $r = 0.151$ ($p < 0.001$).[8]

It is also worth mentioning that liberal views (in both senses) go in line with interest in public life, especially with a habit of following current politics in media, which is important from the point of view of the analyses presented in the next chapters of this book. Those with liberal views would tend to read more about politics and economy, so they have more chance to become opinion-makers for their social environment.

[6] Due to the ordinal character of the variables Spearman's coefficients were calculated.

[7] Index of moral liberalism was constructed based on the respondent's readiness to justify such behaviours as homosexuality, abortion, divorce, having casual sex, and artificial insemination or in-vitro fertilisation. The more of those the respondent justified, the higher value of the index.

[8] Positive sign of Spearman's coefficient means that the more important this goal is, the more right-wing the respondent feels.

4.2 Attitudes Towards International Trade

International trade and trade debates are usually the aspects of public life that gather relatively less public opinion's attention than current politics: nuances of political economy, as well as the issues of international trade, are relatively complex so they usually do not appear in most popular press or TV channels.

The analysts from Pew Research Centre have noticed that most of the world supports globalisation in theory, but there are many doubts once it comes to the details.[9] For example, the aggregated opinion of the inhabitants from 44 countries surveyed in 2014 was that international trade was good (81% said so). They felt it was also good when foreign companies build new factories in their country (74% expressed this opinion). The attitudes were not that uniform when talking about other aspects of international trade—still, the majority (54%) believed that international trade created jobs, but only one in four (26%) agreed that it lowered prices (which is the basic argument raised by the economists when explaining why nations should trade).

In the European countries (and the USA) included in Pew Research's survey in both 2014 and 2018, the positive opinion about international trade did not change much within the period between surveys. When looking from the perspective of those who think that international trade is "very good" or "good", we note the increase in percentages in all surveyed countries and the difference is usually not bigger than 5%. There are two exceptions, however: the United States where the share of having a positive view on international trade increased by 8% and Poland where it increased by 7.5%. We observe more diversity between the countries when considering only the strongest opinion, that is "very good", as seen in Fig. 4.3.

Poland demonstrates a quite high increase in the presented percentage, but at the same time, it has one of the lowest shares of respondents strongly convinced about positive effects of international trade on their country (this percentage was lower only in Italy).

When looking from the perspective of particular economic effects of international trade (level of wages, number of jobs, and level of prices) as perceived by the societies, one can note that in eight of ten studied countries, most respondents believe that international trade leads to job

[9] http://pewrsr.ch/Xc3LEL (accessed November 20th, 2019).

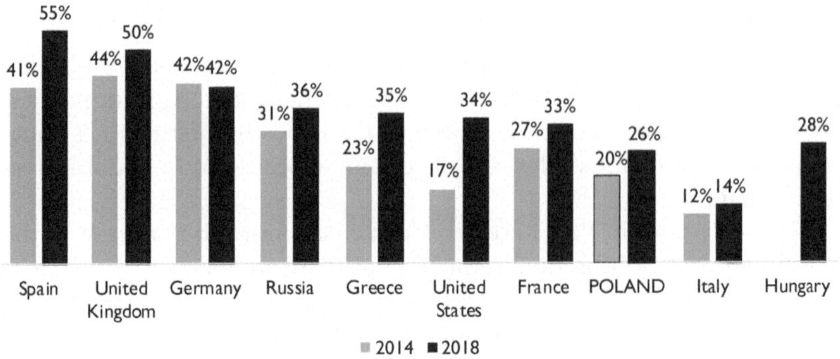

Fig. 4.3 Changes in attitudes towards foreign trade in chosen European countries and the USA between 2014 and 2018. Percentage of those who think foreign trade is "very good". (Data source: Pew Research, 2014 and 2018 (own calculations))

creation. Only in Italy and France, the prevailing opinion is that international trade reduces jobs (Fig. 4.4). Concerning the two other effects, the opinions are not that optimistic. In four countries, the citizens tend to think that international trade decreases wages and in seven that it leads to prices' growth. Poles are pessimistic only in the third of the described effects as they expect a growth of prices rather than their reduction due to international trade.

The three potential effects of international trade can be presented as the international trade perception index that counts the number of positive effects indicated by the respondent. The index takes values from 0 to 3, where 0 means that no positive effects were mentioned and 3 means that the respondent mentioned all three (increasing wages, job creation, and decreasing prices).

Turning to Poland, one notes that its citizens are the most optimistic about the effects of international trade when compared to the countries where the survey was repeated in 2014 and 2018 (Fig. 4.5). The average number of potential positive outcomes indicated by Poles is the greatest and the country noted one of the greatest increases since 2014 (just after the US). The general structure of these attitudes is in line with the one observed globally: 51% of Poles thought that the trade led to job creation (22% said it rather led to job losses), but only 26% believed it reduced prices. It is worth mentioning here that among the countries with the

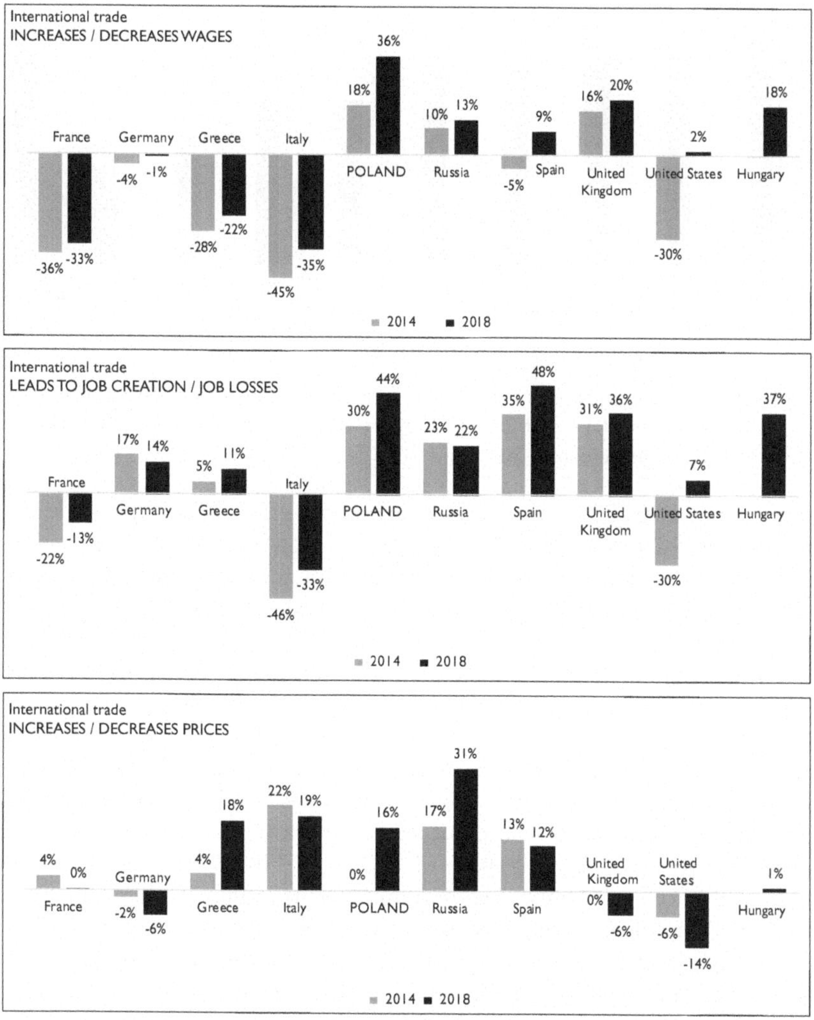

Fig. 4.4 Opinions* about the effects of international trade on wages, jobs, and prices in selected European countries and the USA. * The graphs present "net opinions" that were calculated by deducting percentages of those thinking that "wages decrease" from those who think that "wages increase"; percentages of answers that trade leads to "job losses" were deducted from the percentage of saying that it leads to "job creation" and percentages of those claiming that "prices decrease" were deducted from those saying "prices increase". Hungary did not participate in 2014 survey. (Data source: Pew Research, 2014 and 2018 [own calculations])

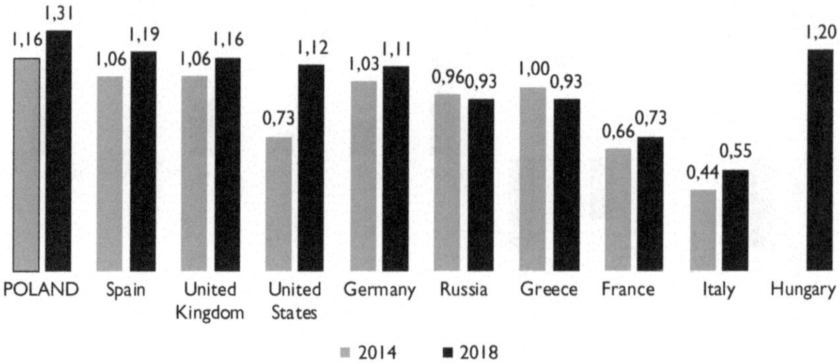

Fig. 4.5 Average number of positive effects of international trade indicated by the respondents in 2014 and 2018. Hungary did not participate in 2014 survey. (Data source: Pew Research, 2014 and 2018 [own calculations])

highest percentage of those opposing positive effect of foreign trade on the number of jobs were mostly those with a high level of GDP per capita: Italy (59% thought it leads to job losses, 13% that it creates jobs), USA (50% for job losses, 20% for creation), and France (49% for job losses, 24% for creation).[10]

In the majority of the countries considered in this analysis, the attitudes towards international trade correlated with satisfaction with the country's economic situation and satisfaction with democracy. The latter correlation appeared insignificant in Poland or very weak in Hungary,[11] while the relation of international trade perception index to the evaluation of economic performance was similar to the one recorded in other countries. This suggests that for a substantial share of Poles and Hungarians international trade is a purely economic phenomenon and its evaluation has very little to do with political attitudes or preferences. In other countries, excluding the UK,[12] the correlation was positive, which means that those satisfied with democracy tended to see more positive outcomes of international trade than those who were dissatisfied.

[10] https://www.pewresearch.org/global/2014/09/16/faith-and-skepticism-about-trade-foreign-investment/ (accessed November 20th, 2019).

[11] Due to ordinal level of measurement in case of satisfaction with democracy, Spearman's correlation coefficients were calculated. Its values were 0.044 (p = 0.18) for Poland and 0.071 (p = 0.03) for Hungary.

[12] In the United Kingdom all the described correlations were insignificant.

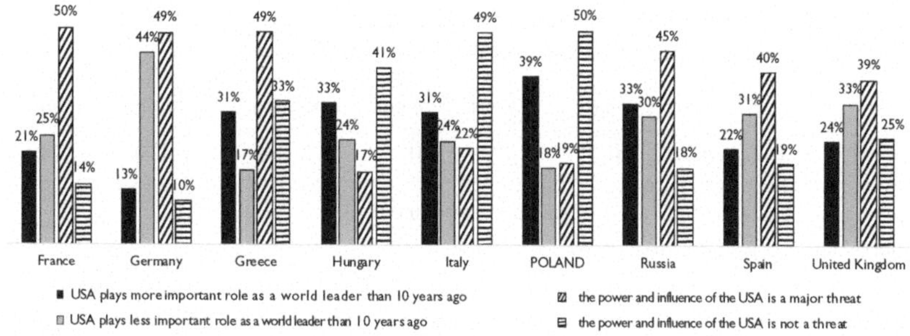

Fig. 4.6 Opinions about the influence of the USA as a world leader in nine European countries. (Data source: Pew Research 2018 (own calculations))

Poland appeared to be the most pro-American among all European countries included in the current analysis. Pew Research Centre asked the respondents in 2018 about their perception of the United States as a world leader. They were to decide whether its role as a world leader role is more important and powerful, less important, or more or less the same as ten years ago. Another question concerned the US's power and influence—the respondents were asked whether this constitutes major threat, minor threat, or not a threat at all for their country. Some of the results are presented in Fig. 4.6.

The results show that inhabitants of Poland, Italy, and Hungary mostly do not consider the power and influence of the United States a threat to their countries. They also think that the international influence of the USA increases over time. This position is substantially different from the one expressed by the Germans who think that the American influence is less than before, but this influence is nevertheless a major threat to their country. Also, the respondents in France, Greece, and Russia are afraid of the US's power and influence in the world.

Inhabitants of European countries do not really perceive the world as divided between Russia and the USA. The correlation coefficients between the opinions on the threat resulting from Russia's power and influence and the one of the USA are positive in all countries included in this analysis. This means that those who feel that the USA is a major threat tend to think the same about Russia—and feeling no threat from Russia goes in line with similar opinions about the US threat (Table 4.2).

In Poland, the correlation is the weakest among all the countries under study because there is a substantial share of inhabitants who clearly

Table 4.2 Correlation coefficients between the opinions about the threat from the power and influence of Russia and the USA (2018)

Italy	*Greece*	*France*	*Spain*	*United Kingdom*	*Hungary*	*Germany*	*Poland*
0.471	0.454	0.368	0.277	0.245	0.198	0.174	0.149

Spearman's coefficients. All of them are significant at $p < 0.001$

Data source: Pew Research 2018 (own calculations)

distinguish between the two powers and are afraid more of Russia than of the USA: 68% of Poles see Russia as the major threat and only 19% perceive the US in that way. There is also 31% of those who see the major threat from Russia and no threat at all from the USA, while the opposite opinion (major threat from the USA and no threat from Russia) is expressed by only 1% of those surveyed. Considering it, a substantial percentage of Polish citizens may perceive good relationships with the USA as a security measure against potential threats from Russia.

4.3 Attitudes Towards TTIP and Globalisation

The previous analyses showed that citizens of the EU members are quite diverse in their opinions and perceptions of the USA's role and position in the world politics and economy. These attitudes must affect the perception of TTIP, an FTA between the European Union and the USA.

The issue was included in several Eurobarometer Surveys. The last one asking about the FTA was conducted in 2017, two months after the negotiations had been officially suspended (Table 4.3).

In 2014, 2015, and 2016 when the TTIP was for the most part still on the agenda of the negotiators, the greatest opposition towards TTIP, apart from Austrians (2015: 67% and 2016: 70% "against"), were Germans (51% and 59% "against") and Luxembourgers (49% and 50% "against""), whereas Lithuanians (79% and 77% "for"), Romanians (78% and 77% "for""), and Irish (77% and 70% "for") were among the biggest supporters of TTIP. That was not a perfect reflection of the geographical distribution of free trade attitudes across the EU. Nevertheless, Polish enthusiasm towards free trade turned out to be almost bulletproof while expressed as quite high support for TTIP (71% "for" in 2015 although with a decline to only 59% in 2016).

Table 4.3 Distribution of the respondents' answers to the question: Do you support or not a free trade and investment agreement between the EU and the US? (Total for all EU members)

	Autumn 2014	*Spring 2015*	*Autumn 2015*	*Spring 2016*	*Autumn 2016*	*Spring 2017*
For (%)	58	56	53	51	53	54
Against (%)	25	28	32	34	34	32
Do not know (%)	17	16	15	15	13	14

Source: European Commission, Standard Eurobarometer 87, 86, 85, 84, 83

Map 4.1 presents the percentage of support for TTIP in 2017 in the EU member states.

Is there more about EU citizens' attitudes towards TTIP hidden in the socio-demographic qualities? To answer this question, let us focus on Poland and its closest EU neighbours—among which Germany belongs to the most populous and influential member states.

As we can see in Table 4.4, there were no big differences between male and female response distribution patterns in 2017. In Poland and the Czech Republic, shares of men that supported TTIP vaguely overcame supporting majorities of women, which was the opposite tendency for the German "against" male and female majorities. In Slovakia, women expressed their support for the agreement slightly more frequently than men.

Moreover, the younger the citizens, the more open they were towards TTIP, a universal trend in Central-Eastern Europe. Germans' opinions did not fit in this pattern—there the most supportive group was the one of 35–44 year-olds.

More advanced education levels corresponded to more incisive views on TTIP if only "for" views were to be considered, but it also works for German "against". Both "for" and "against" appeared to be "educated guesses", although contradictory.

In Poland, the rural areas' inhabitants tended to be against the agreement more frequently than those living in urban areas. In Germany, the tendency was just the opposite: more support in villages, less—in towns (in large towns only one third supported TTIP).

It seems that the Polish opinions about TTIP are in line with a generally positive attitude towards Americans. Since 1993, when these attitudes

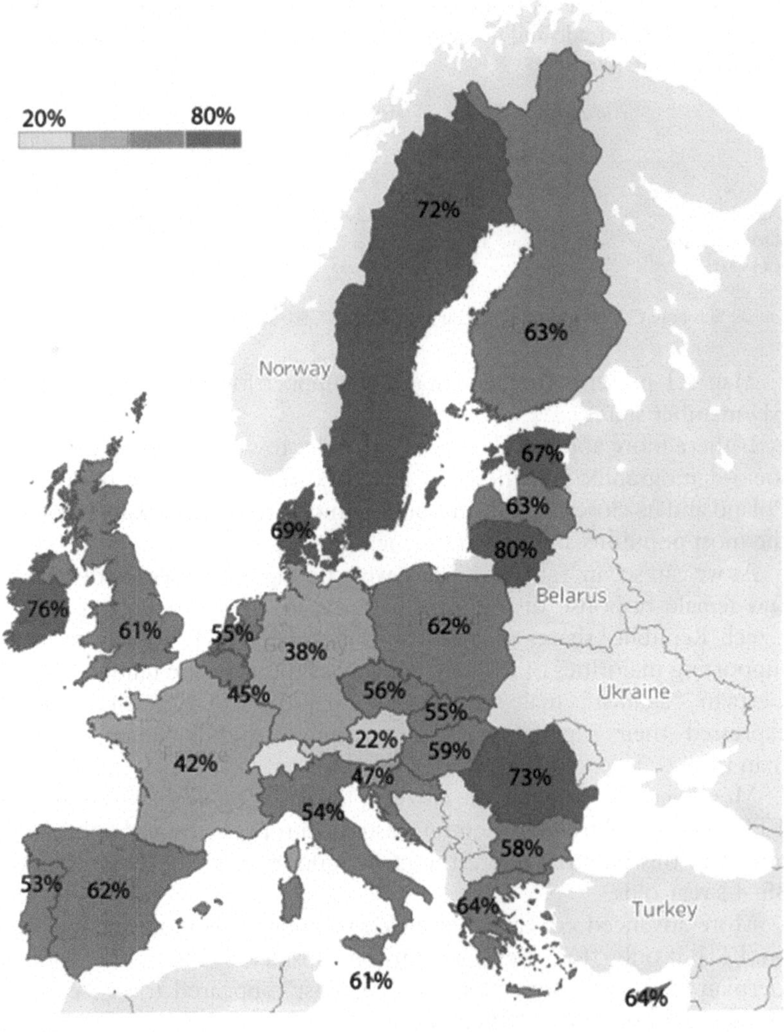

Map 4.1 Support for Free Trade Agreement between the European Union and the USA. (Data Source: Eurobarometer 87.3. 2017 (https://doi.org/10.4232/1.12847), own calculations.) Map created with Tableau Public Software

Table 4.4 Attitudes towards free trade and investment agreement between the EU and USA in four countries broken by socio-demographic characteristics

	Germany		*Czech Republic*		*Poland*		*Slovakia*	
	For (%)	*Against (%)*	*For (%)*	*Against (%)*	*For (%)*	*Against (%)*	*For (%)*	*Against (%)*
Total	38	52	56	35	62	21	55	30
Gender								
Men	39	54	60	35	63	24	53	35
Women	36	50	53	36	62	19	56	26
Age group								
15–24	36	56	64	31	68	21	71	17
25–34	37	53	68	26	63	23	58	27
35–44	41	50	57	36	69	18	56	28
45–54	36	57	59	36	62	24	56	34
55–64	38	53	49	40	59	22	49	35
65+	38	49	45	41	57	19	52	29
Age when finished education								
<15	35	50	38	58	49	21	47	28
16–19	41	50	55	34	61	21	53	32
20+	36	55	60	34	66	21	58	27
Still studying	31	60	72	24	68	21	79	14
Type of community								
Rural area or village	42	47	61	33	57	26	49	37
Small or middle town	36	54	51	39	69	13	62	20
Large town	33	56	60	32	64	21	51	36

Data source: Eurobarometer 87.3. 2017 (https://doi.org/10.4232/1.12847), own calculations

started to be recorded, the level of sympathy stays around 50% (43% in 2018) and substantially exceeds the level of antipathy, which have usually been no more than 20% (14% in 2018). Also, the evaluation of bilateral relations between Poland and the US is a net positive. There is no data exactly from the time when the Eurobarometer survey was conducted, but before and after that, that is in 2016 and 2018, 32% and 47%, respectively, though the relationship was good,[13] while only 8% and 5%, respectively, perceived it as bad.

[13] CBOS, Report no. 47/2019.

The TTIP and CETA agreements are widely perceived as signs of progressing globalisation of the economy. This process itself seems controversial from the perspective of its impact on ordinary people's economic situation. Many authors argue that globalisation leads to expansion of welfare states, caused by stronger than before feeling of economic insecurity within large groups of societies, which governments then compensate in various ways (the compensation hypothesis). A comprehensive overview of the literature on the relationship between increasing globalisation and the welfare state can be found, for example in the article by Stefanie Walter (2010). The interconnection mechanism could be presented differently, but nearly all of the authors agree that globalisation raises the feeling of economic insecurity in the society.

This seems not to be the case in Poland—Poles tend to see more positive than negative sides of globalisation (Fig. 4.7). The Public Opinion Research Centre (CBOS) asked about this issue three times within 13 years and the results demonstrate growing, not decreasing, percentage of positive attitudes towards the globalising economy. The question's wording was the following: *The economies of various countries are increasingly interconnected and dependent on each other. There are many international companies that work in multiple countries and the economy develops freely above the state borders. Would you say this phenomenon is positive or negative?*

Answering a similar question in Eurobarometer 87.3 (2017), Poles confirmed their positive attitude towards globalisation: 13% of them *totally agreed* and 45% *agreed* with the statement that *globalisation is an opportunity for economic growth.* The respondents were mostly consistent in their opinions about globalisation as these answers correlated with the position

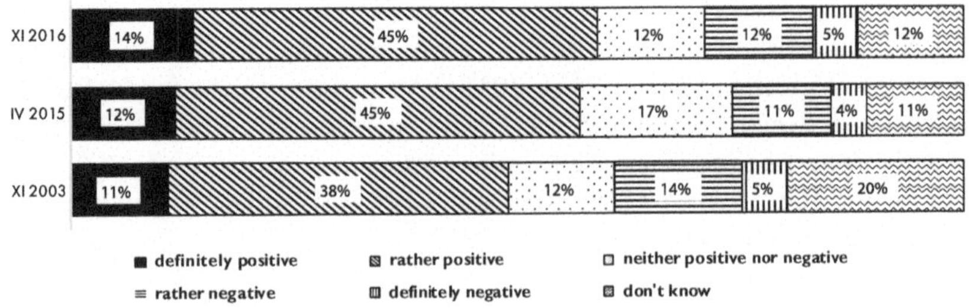

Fig. 4.7 Poles' attitudes towards the processes of globalisation of the economy. (Source: CBOS Report 167/2016 (www.cbos.pl))

on the TTIP agreement. Among those who totally agreed with the globalisation statement, nearly 80% supported the agreement and among those who disagreed the agreement opponent prevailed (46% against and 35% for the agreement).

The dominant opinion in the Polish society is that globalisation is an opportunity for economic development, which in turn is believed to be of the highest importance for Poland. The cited CBOS study showed that majority of respondents saw the positive impact of globalisation processes on most of the spheres of life they were asked about (Polish economy, Polish enterprises, consumers, employees, and agriculture[14]). The globalisation processes can also be perceived in Poland as a chance for the society to become a part of the western world, a dream maintained by many generations of Poles, and a dream that—in the eyes of many—has not come true so far (Grzymski 2016). Such a way of thinking about globalisation might be one of the causes of somehow paradoxical tendency in the Polish society, where the political left more often sees positive outcomes of globalisation for the Polish economy than the other sides of the political arena.[15]

Poles are also enthusiastic about the membership of their country in the European Union. This attitude has many nuances as not all Poles accept the cultural agenda of the EU (see Konieczna-Sałamatin and Sawicka 2020). However, on the general level the support is very high: in 2019 almost everyone (91%) positively answered the direct question "do you support membership of Poland in the European Union"? The dynamics of the answers within the last 25 years are presented in Fig. 4.8.

The above figure shows that the start of negotiations on accession in the mid-1990s and making the membership perspective more real led to the reduction of support. After joining the EU in 2004, the predicted by many "post-accession shock" did not come, which substantially reduced the uncertainty and fears connected with the membership. Visible positive effects of the membership that soon appeared caused the increase in support. Since 2006—with one exception in 2013—the support has never dropped below 80%.

Other data, such as EVS, demonstrate that the confidence in the EU as the institution of public life positively correlates with support for private

[14] In the case of agriculture, the positive impact was indicated more often than negative one (41% and 38% respectively); however, it was not the majority who saw positive impact.

[15] CBOS, Report no. 167/2016, p. 8.

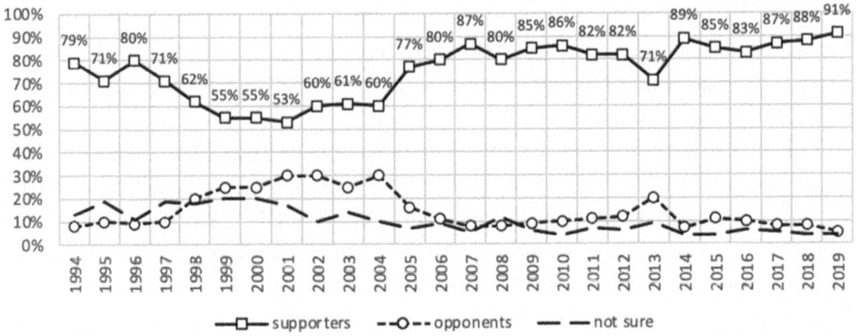

Fig. 4.8 Percentages of the EU membership supporters in Poland (1994–2019). (Source: CBOS (Centre for Public Opinion Research, www.cbos.pl), Report no. 59/2019)

ownership in business[16] (those who trust the EU also tend to support private ownership in the industry), which suggests that Poles adequately perceive the economic position of the EU as a strong supporter of free markets. At the same time, those expressing a higher level of confidence in the EU tend to place themselves closer to the left-wing of the political spectrum.[17]

4.4 Summarising Remarks

As a summary of the findings presented in this chapter, we should underline that TTIP, the free trade and investment agreement between the EU and USA, is perceived as an element of the ongoing globalisation. This seems to be true for both the European (including Polish) and American societies. The evaluation of this agreement strongly depends on general attitudes towards globalisation and how these processes are perceived to affect the countries' economic situation.

The Polish society quite widely shares the image of living on the "underdeveloped" side of Europe and agrees that Poland is still "catching

[16] Spearman's correlation is 0.165 ($p < 0.001$).

[17] Spearman's correlation is 0.309 ($p < 0.001$). The scale of confidence is reversed: 1 means the greatest trust and 4 the greatest distrust. On the left-right scale 1 means "left" and 10 means "right" (and all the numbers in between are to express less radical position).

up" with the world's more successful parts. The widespread belief that economic growth is still one of the most important aims of the country together with a high level of legitimisation of income inequalities suggests that Poles are generally quite optimistic about their chances to finally succeed in this process and believe it is possible to do by individual effort. Globalisation, international trade, and other forms of international economic activity are seen as opportunities to develop faster and get closer to "civilised" West. That is why the expectations of the outcomes of globalisation are in Poland generally optimistic and the attitudes towards the USA and its position in the world are generally positive—as the USA is one of the symbols of "the West". This is probably true—at least to some extent—also when talking about other Central-East European societies.

It is also good to remember that Polish society is not completely uniform in its perception of the integrational processes, which are the element and consequences of globalisation. Since the beginning of the Polish transition in 1989, the support for getting integrated with the Western rather than the Eastern centre was quite high, as illustrated on the graph showing the level of support for the EU membership. However, even if the membership is not questioned, the diversity of opinions arises around understanding of the "idea of Europe". Konieczna-Sałamatin and Sawicka (2020) have shown that European integration can be presented as "triple modernization", in which institutional and economic aspects are mostly not questioned, while cultural (axiological) one raises some doubts, especially in the conservative parts of the society. This conservative part of the Polish society becomes sensitive to the arguments questioning the value of Poland getting close to Western societies and cultures because of the mentioned cultural reasons. They understand European identity in a narrow sense—strongly connected with Christian religion, so they are rather reluctant to accept any processes that may change it, such as immigration from non-Christian parts of the world or giving the LGBT people equal access to marriage. At the same time, they would be ready to listen to emotional arguments against any form of strengthening the ties between Poland and the West when these arguments refer to such cultural values as tolerance for otherness, LGBT rights, and so on.

References

Domański, Henryk, & Aleksandra Dukaczewska. (1995). Is Individualism in Poland Still Alive? *Social Science Information*, 34(3): 389–412. https://doi.org/10.1177/053901895034003002.

Grzymski, J. (2016). Powrót Do Europy—Polski Dyskurs. Wyznaczanie Perspektywy Krytycznej. Warszawa: Oficyna Wydawnicza Uczelni Łazarskiego.

Hofstede, Geert, Geert Jan Hofstede, & Michael Minkov. (2010). *Culture and Organizations. Software of the Mind. I.* 3rd ed. McGraw Hill.

Konieczna-Sałamatin, J., & Sawicka, M. (2020). The East of the West, or the West of the East? Attitudes toward the European Union and European Integration in Poland after 2008. *East European Politics and Societies: And Cultures*, 35(June), 1–21. https://doi.org/10.1177/0888325420926633.

Marody, Mira. (2017). Wartości w świecie postspołecznym [Values in Post-social World]. *Zarządzanie Publiczne*, 1(1/39), 49–55. https://doi.org/10.15678/ZP.2017.39.1.05.

Marody, Mira. (2019). Transformations of Polish Society. *Social Research: An International Quarterly*, 86(1): 57–81.

Touraine, A. (2014). *After the Crisis*. Polity Press.

Walter, S. (2010). Globalization and the Welfare State: Testing the Microfoundations of the Compensation Hypothesis. *International Studies Quarterly*, 54(2): 403–426. https://doi.org/10.1111/j.1468-2478.2010.00593.x.

Wojcik, A. D., Cislak, A., & Schmidt, P. (2019, July 24). Left and Right Political Orientation in Eastern and Western Europe. https://doi.org/10.31234/osf.io/a2jxf.

CHAPTER 5

Academic Expert Knowledge on Free Trade

Abstract The chapter consists of three distinctive sections. First, it provides a demonstration of how the Polish academic literature on the effects of Free Trade Agreements (FTAs) compares to that in English, French, German, and Italian. It shows that the Polish outputs follow patterns similar to those in the other languages and makes a proposition that the Polish research literature could be representative of that in other countries. Second, it analyses 51 research publications on FTAs published in Polish between 1995 and 2019. We note that the sentiment of the majority of outputs is unequivocally favourable towards free trade. Third, we construct the Expert Knowledge Dictionary (EKD) of 1540 terms frequently encountered in the academic literature. It is then used in Chap. 6 to conduct the content analysis of the Polish internet news sources and examine the extent of expert knowledge contained in them.

Keywords Expert knowledge • Academic literature • Expert Knowledge Dictionary • Comparative meta-analysis

Unsurprisingly, FTAs draw a considerable amount of attention from experts such as researchers and policy analysts. Ideally, evidence provided by experts should drive policymaking as well as the public discourse on issues such as free trade and associated deals. In this chapter, we analyse the expert voices on FTAs in Polish-language internet sources. In Chaps.

B. Gawrońska-Nowak et al., *Trade Wins or Trade Wars*,
https://doi.org/10.1007/978-3-030-76997-0_5

6 and 7 we will compare and contrast those voices with the sentiment and emotions contained in articles published in popular Polish news portals and readers' reactions.

The current chapter is divided into three distinctive sections. First, we provide a simple demonstration of how the Polish academic literature on the effects of the seven agreements compares to the literature in English, which is the lingua franca of modern scholarship, and three other European languages. By focusing on descriptive analysis looking at numbers of publications over time, we show that the Polish outputs follow patterns similar to those of the research discourse in the English language, albeit at a much smaller scale. This seems to be true also for research outputs published in French, German, and Italian. We make a weak proposition that, judging by the magnitude and time dynamics of academic publications, our analysis of the Polish research literature presented in this book may be representative of the broader expert discourse on the issues of the FTAs in the non-English, European academic literature. Second, we construct a database of research publications on any of the seven FTAs published in the Polish language between 1995 and 2019 and synthesise the expert judgement contained in a large sample of 51 academic articles. This comparative meta-analysis allows us to determine and describe the experts' attitudes and sentiments towards the FTAs. In Chap. 6 we will investigate whether those attitudes feed into opinions and sentiments expressed by journalists and readers in their articles and comments. Third, using the same sample of research articles, we construct the Expert Knowledge Dictionary (EKD) which will be used in Chap. 6 to conduct the content analysis of the Polish internet news sources and examine the extent of expert knowledge contained in them. When analysing the expert literature, we keep track of time to observe how expert attitudes towards the FTAs changed over time. In particular, we are interested to see whether there was a shift in the attitudes around the Great Recession of 2008.

5.1 How the Polish-Language Literature Compares to Its European Counterparts

To show that the volumes of research outputs in the Polish language follow trends and patterns similar to those in other languages, we begin by comparing the volume of FTA books published in Polish to those published in English. To that end, we use the catalogues of the National

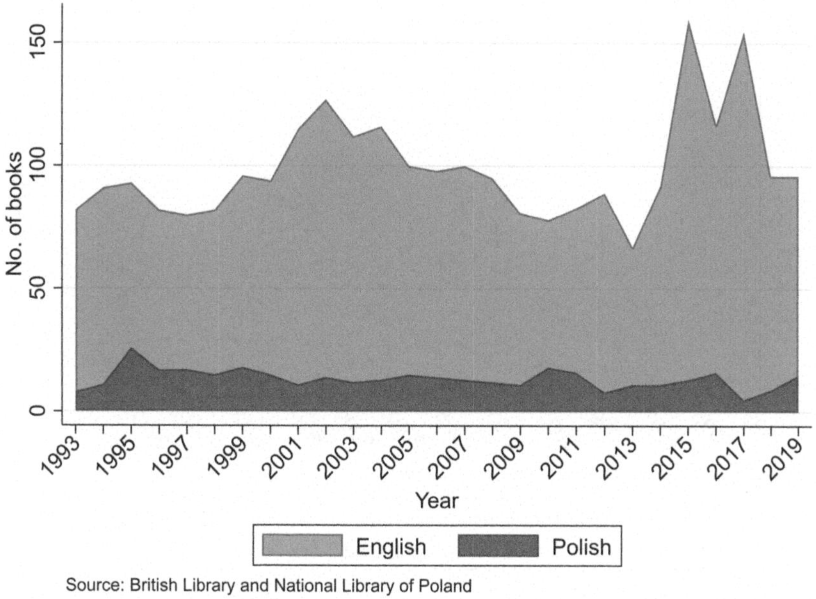

Fig. 5.1 Books on FTAs: English versus Polish

Library of Poland and the British Library to pull the numbers of books on the topic of any of the studied agreements published in each year from 1993 until 2019.[1] Figure 5.1 shows that, as expected, the number of books published in Polish is only a fraction of the English publications. On average, there were 13 books published in Polish[2] and 92 in English per year. There appears to be a small spike in the number of books published in both languages in 1995, which was most likely fuelled by the recent establishment of the WTO and creation of NAFTA and CEFTA. Following this period, the supply of books in Polish falls and remains fairly stable, whereas the English supply is on an upward trajectory until 2002. We observe a pronounced spike in English publications between 2014 and 2017 when the large deals, that is TPP, CETA, and TTIP, capture the

[1] We search the catalogues for publications which contain any of the keywords, CEFTA, CETA, GATT, WTO, NAFTA, TPP, or TTIP, in the subject, title, description, or abstract fields and are published in either English (British Library) or Polish (National Library of Poland).

[2] Some of the books are translations of books from English or other languages.

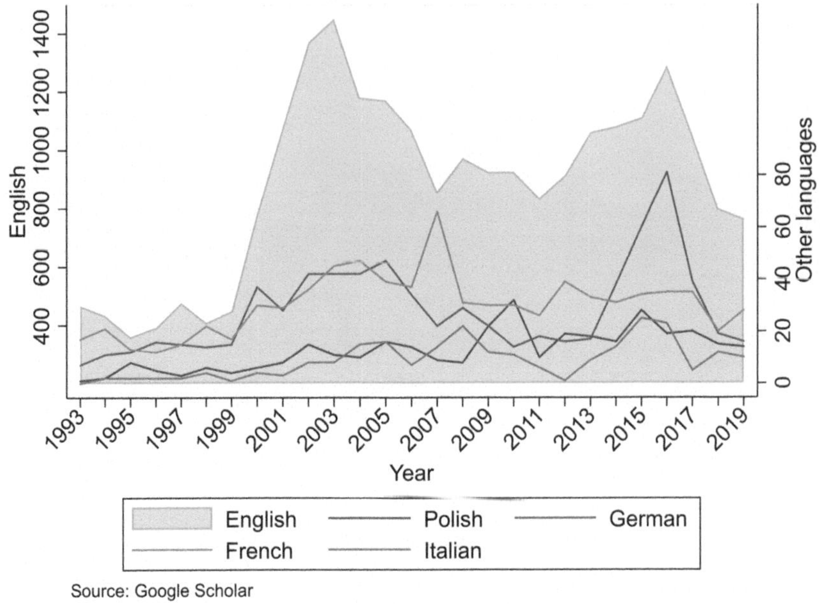

Fig. 5.2 Academic articles in Polish, English, German, French, and Italian

international agenda. Interestingly, this increased interest is not reflected in the Polish publishing as the number of books falls to only five in 2017, the lowest level since 1992.[3]

Next, we compare the numbers of research publications listed in Google Scholar and published in Polish, English, German, French, or Italian, including journal articles, books, and working papers.[4] Figure 5.2 shows a large disparity between the numbers of publications in English and any of the other languages. Therefore, we display the corresponding numbers on two separate axes. On average, there were 13 research publications

[3] Arguably, the drop in the number of books published by Polish researchers might have been a consequence of policy changes. The new evaluation policy that favours academic journal articles over books was introduced in 2018 but the research community had known in advance that the changes would be introduced. Thus, the academics might have started adjusting their research pipeline and portfolio already in the mid-2010s.

[4] We search Google Scholar for publications which contain any of the keywords listed above in the title field.

concerning any of the discussed FTAs in Polish a year[5]; this compares to approximately 30 in each German and French, and only 9 in Italian. These statistics look pale compared to the average number of publications in English at 877 outputs a year.[6] Compared to the 1990s, research outputs in all languages doubled and tripled in the twenty-first century, which reflects the policymakers and experts' growing interest in free trade and the topical nature of FTAs in the 2000s. This is most pronounced in the 2010s when the new large trade deals such as CETA, TTIP, and TPP surfaced to the economic policy and, therefore, research agenda.

A visual inspection of Fig. 5.2 suggests that the volumes of research publications in the five languages seem to follow similar patterns, albeit with some regional variations and possible time lags. The correlation coefficients between the Polish outputs and outputs in the other languages range from 0.35 for French to 0.57 for English. The greatest similarity is observed between German and English, and French and English with correlation coefficients of 0.74 and 0.7, respectively. The pairwise correlations among the volumes of outputs in all languages are statistically significant at the 5% significance level, except the Polish-French correlation coefficient which is statistically significant at 8% significance level.

So far, we have seen that although being much lower, the numbers of Polish research outputs are positively correlated with those in English, the lingua franca of modern research, and three other European languages. But how does their content compare? Without going into detail, we observe that the Polish research outputs appear to be more qualitative and descriptive and less quantitative when compared to the mainstream trade literature in English. In the following section, we explore that claim and take a closer look at the content of a sample of Polish research articles.

[5] Google Scholar is an imperfect tool for measuring the quantities of research outputs but it appears to be the most popular and most convenient tool for searching for research publications. The number 13 is the same as the average number of books listed in the Polish National Library's catalogue. Interestingly, our Google Scholar search results for the Polish language did not return any books. Thus, 13 is the number of articles and working papers published in Polish.

[6] Some of the English language outputs are written by Polish researchers and published in Poland-based journals. We focus on the Polish-language publications only due to their greater accessibility to the expert and non-expert audiences in Poland.

5.2 Polish FTA Literature: The Sample

To construct our expert content database, we turn to Google Scholar and search for outputs published in the Polish language between 1994 and 2019. We identify 198 research articles and working papers that contain the name or abbreviation of any of the seven FTAs in their title. Out of those, we select 51 publications which form a sample to be investigated in more detail in the current and subsequent sections. Our selection process follows four principles. First, mindful of the potential impact of the Great Recession of 2008 on the public perception of the global and domestic economies, economic policy, trade, and globalisation, we want to have a good cross-section of articles published in the years to 2008 and from 2009 onward. Such a division of our sample into two sub-periods should allow us to detect whether the expert opinion on FTAs was affected by the major economic crisis and the ensuing re-evaluation of economic theories. This distinction is also preserved in Chap. 6 where we capture the Great Recession's impact on the wider public opinion.

Second, we ensure that each of the FTAs is represented in our sample and that the share of articles about each agreement is a balanced representation of all articles identified through Google Scholar. Table 5.1 summarises the distribution of the sample across the FTAs and the two sub-periods. Since some of the agreements have reached the agenda only towards the end of the period covered by our research, for example TTIP

Table 5.1 Share of publications by period and FTA

Period	*1994–2019*		*1994–2008*		*2009–2019*	
FTA[a]	*Selected sample*	*Google Scholar results*	*Selected sample*	*Google Scholar results*	*Selected sample*	*Google Scholar results*
GATT or WTO	37%	51%	50%	55%	32%	48%
CEFTA	12%	17%	36%	33%	3%	3%
NAFTA	16%	11%	14%	12%	16%	10%
CETA	8%	6%			11%	11%
TPP	4%	2%			5%	4%
TTIP	29%	15%			41%	29%
Number of publications	51	198	14	93	37	105

[a]Some publications mention multiple FTAs in their titles and thus the percentages do not add up to 100%.

and CETA, the selected sample inevitably contains proportionally more outputs published in the post-2008 period. This balancing act, which accounts for the emerging of new agreements and "fading" of others, namely CEFTA, prevents us from constructing a sample in which percentage shares of FTAs follow closely the shares returned from the Google Scholar search. Notably, the share of publications with a focus on GATT and WTO appears to remain fairly stable throughout the two periods—this is because they are often used as a starting point and a benchmark in the discussion of the newer FTAs.

Third, the selected sample takes into consideration the frequency of publishing FTA-related articles by individual authors. The 198 outputs found on Google Scholar have very dispersed authorship—they are authored or co-authored by 143 individual researchers giving an average of 1.5 publications per individual. Thus, the names of the majority of researchers (103 authors) appear only on a single FTA-related output. Only five authors published five or more articles and forty had more than one relevant output. Our sample reflects the high level of authorship dispersion as the 51 outputs represent work of 52 individual researchers, 11 of whom produced more than one output. To ensure an adequate plurality of voices, we include no more than three publications by one author within the sample.

Finally, we also consider the publication outlets, that is journals and working paper series, in which the outputs are published. The Google Scholar results are attributed to 53 individual outlets[7], but only three produced more than ten relevant publications between 1994 and 2019. We mimic that multiplicity of sources by including publications from 31 outlets and a proportionally larger number of entries from journals that are more prolific in the FTA studies. Nearly two-fifths of the 51 articles in the sample are published in outlets with only a single FTA-related publication in the analysed period, whereas the remaining 32 articles come from outlets with multiple FTA publications. Such an approach to constructing the sample should ensure that it represents the plurality of expert voices in the Polish trade debate as journals and working papers in Poland are usually directly linked to universities or research institutes and often are the main channel for dissemination of research for their employees. Thus, we

[7] In cases when an outlet may have changed its title during the analysed period but otherwise maintained continuity of its publishing activities, we count outputs published before and after the title change as coming from one entity.

ensure that our sample represents a wide range of academic centres but, at the same time, we allow a proportionately larger number of entries from outlets which frequently publish articles on FTAs. Such outlets are likely to be more influential in the broader debate on FTAs for two reasons. First, they tend to be formed around research centres that employ relatively large numbers of researchers specialising in FTAs and who may form "local centres of excellence" in this area, for example the Universities of Economics in Wrocław and Kraków. Second, their reputation for studies on international trade is likely to attract more attention from both researchers and pundits.

Following those four principles, we construct a sample consisting of publications distributed across years, FTAs, authors, and outlets, and should provide a fair representation of the expert sentiment. The Polish literature's striking feature is that it is overwhelmingly descriptive and often limited to plain reporting on developments in trade negotiations or analytical results published elsewhere. Out of the 51 articles in our sample, only four contain some form of original quantitative analysis and 12 are somewhat analytical. The remainder is purely descriptive, often merely expressing authors' opinions or summarising official FTA-related documents' contents. The sentiment of the majority of outputs is unequivocally favourable towards free trade: 37 articles are enthusiastic about the FTAs at hand, and generally pro-globalisation, while only seven are sceptical or openly negative in their evaluation of the impacts of the discussed agreements. Only 14 articles contain direct references to the effect of the FTAs for Poland, and 17 outputs consider more than one FTA in their discussion.

The 51 articles in the sample cover a broad variety of issues. The most common theme is the discussion of FTAs' general economic impacts and effect on trade flows (15 articles). The implications for the Polish food and agricultural sector are the focus of 13 articles, with four of them tackling the controversies of GMO in farming. The comparatively large amount of attention paid specifically to agriculture (the next two most frequently discussed industries are chemicals and services, with two articles each) is expected as Poland is a major exporter of food and agricultural products. Further 12 articles offer a general overview of one of the FTAs' rules, whereas the rest touch on topics such as the EU integration, the Great Recession, trade dispute, and security, among others.

5.3 Expected Effects of FTAs

In this section, we take a closer look at the content of the analysed academic literature and arguments it raises in favour or against the FTAs. This review of experts' sentiment or opinions has a two-fold purpose. First, we attempt to establish whether there is a clear and coherent academic expert judgement on the expected effects of the FTAs and the role they play in the international and domestic economy. Second, and more importantly, is the synthesis of the key expert assertions and arguments that inform our analysis of popular news outlets and readers' comments in Chap. 6. Logically, we need to draw the landscape of views expressed by academic experts before investigating whether they feed into the broader public debate. As in the previous section, we maintain the distinction between outputs published before and after the Great Recession of 2008 to determine whether it had a discernible impact on experts' attitudes towards trade deals.

To complete the task at hand, we perform a detailed review of the content of 51 academic outputs in our sample. In each case, we note down any benefits, costs, opportunities, and threats indicated by authors. By benefits, we understand direct and positive expected consequences of signing a trade deal, for example increases in exports. In contrast, opportunities refer to favourable or advantageous circumstances indirectly created by trade deals which are likely to lead to positive social, political, or economic outcomes in the future. For example, trade deals may promote greater trust among nations and enhance political cooperation, promoting peace, stability, and thus economic growth and development. Arguably, the line between benefits and opportunities may sometimes become blurry but, nonetheless, both categories represent positive expected outcomes of free trade deals.

In contrast, costs and threats capture the adverse effects of FTAs. Costs are a direct consequence of the trade deal and represent its expected and negative impacts on the domestic economy or society, which in our context may refer to legal costs of implementing provisions of the deal, loss of sectors or jobs which are not competitive in international markets, but also sacrificing or forgoing a degree of control over domestic regulation and industries. In general, costs should be known and factored in the decision-making process of ratifying a trade deal. Finally, threats are linked to the provisions of trade deals that may generate damages, adverse effects, or costs in the future but cannot be foreseen or evaluated when the deal is introduced, such as increases in social inequalities, pollution, or increased vulnerability to external economic shocks. They may also be linked to poor planning and inability to predict consequences of unclear or imprecise rules within the FTA that in the future may raise interpretations causing damages to the signatory's economy, security, sovereignty, or society.

Figure 5.3 shows the results of the synthesis of benefits, costs, threats, and opportunities of FTAs discussed in the Polish academic literature. The numbers in the parentheses shown in the figure provide the counts of how many research outputs within our sample mention each factor. A cursory glance at Fig. 5.3 reveals that the benefits of FTAs are much more frequently discussed than their costs. Out of 51 articles in our sample, 47 highlight at least one positive aspect, that is a benefit or an opportunity, and only 25 outputs take note of any negative aspect. Overall, the balance of opinion appears to be favourable to the FTAs: only half of the articles mention any negative consequences of FTAs and three-quarters, 37 articles, list more positives than negatives.

There is no surprise that the most frequently indicated consequence of signing an FTA is boosting trade flows, a benefit whose importance appears constant throughout the analysed period. Within our sample, 23 articles explicitly point at increases in exports and imports as a desirable consequence of signing a trade deal. This is followed by the closely connected benefits of improved access to foreign markets, standardisation of trade rules, and reduction of non-tariff barriers to trade. The latter two gain significance in the post-2008 literature. Interestingly, the reduction of tariffs is only the tenth most frequently cited benefit of FTAs, noted in nine articles. This shows that with tariffs being already at low levels, their elimination has not been seen as the main target for the modern FTAs, focusing on other elements of the trade environment such as regulatory barriers, investors' rights, and dispute resolution.

The most frequently cited benefits of trade deals point towards increasing the ease of trade among nations which, indeed, is an immediate purpose of a trade deal. Nonetheless, reading the literature, it is difficult to escape an impression that boosting trade volumes is an end in itself rather than a means to achieving other ends, such as greater prosperity within society, higher living standards, or poverty reduction. In fairness, the articles do not limit their perspective only to the gains for importers and exporters, but also note consequences for the wider economy and society, albeit less frequently. For example, there is an expectation of accelerated GDP growth, rising incomes and wealth, creation of new jobs, and

BENEFITS

- increasing trade flows (23)
- access to foreign markets (18)
- standardisation of trade rules (16)
- reducing non-tariff barriers (15)
- enhancing competitiveness (12)
- economic (GDP) growth (11)
- boosting investment flows (10)
- stability and reduced uncertainty (10)
- greater geopolitical power (10)
- reducing tariffs (9)
- consumer welfare (8)
- improving resolution of disputes (7)
- integration into the global economy (6)
- increasing incomes/wealth (4)
- boosting employment (4)
- innovation and technology transfer (2)

COSTS

- weakened food safety (10)
- letting foreign competition into domestic markets (8)
- worse employment conditions (8)
- loss of control over domestic markets and trading standards (5)
- reduced public health provision (4)
- limits on government intervention in domestic markets (3)
- job losses in some sectors (3)
- costly legal changes (3)
- cost of structural adjustments (2)

OPPORTUNITIES

- beneficial environment for economic development (16)
- encouraging political cooperation (4)
- building trust among nations (2)
- promoting structural reforms (2)
- better allocation of resources (1)
- growth of international corporations (1)
- poverty reduction (1)
- mitigating economic crises (1)
- ease of profit transfers (1)
- trade diversification (1)
- international competition in services (1)

THREATS

- GMO and hormone-fed animals (9)
- inadequate dispute resolution (8)
- corporate power over governments (7)
- worsening environmental conditions (5)
- particular national interests (5)
- deteriorating democracy (4)
- deteriorated consumer rights (4)
- rising inequality (3)
- imports from low-wage countries (2)
- higher exports raise domestic prices (2)
- mismanaged structural adjustments (2)
- jobs moving abroad (2)
- marketisation of public services (2)
- vulnerability to shocks in foreign markets (1)
- corporate profits transferred abroad (1)

Fig. 5.3 Benefits, costs, opportunities, and threats indicated in the research outputs improved consumer welfare thanks to lower prices and greater choice of products and services. However, these issues receive far less attention, and there is virtually no discussion about how to compensate losers from international trade or share the newly generated wealth within the economy and society.

Several, mostly post-2008, articles note some less tangible benefits of FTAs such as reduced uncertainty and greater stability, both in doing business and international relations, as well as signatories' greater geopolitical power and ability to influence the international agenda. The latter is particularly often mentioned when discussing TTIP: the authors see the US–EU trade deal as a way to assert the West's dominance in the international economy, dictate the global trading standards, and determine the direction of future growth (e.g. Dunin-Wąsowicz, 2014; Majchrowska, 2015; Oręziak, 2015; Nacewska-Twardowska, 2017; Czarny et al., 2017). Innovation and technology transfer appear at the bottom of the benefits list, and only two publications pay them a meaningful amount of attention (Kuźnar, 2004; Ambroziak, 2016). This is rather surprising because Poland as a developing country has greatly benefited from an inflow of modern technologies and innovations which propped up entire industries, for example car manufacturing, and was often possible thanks to direct investment from developed countries.

The list of positive consequences of the FTAs is complemented by several opportunities. Nearly a third of the articles see trade deals as a chance for creating a beneficial environment for economic development. This rather vague phrase may summarise the opportunities and benefits already specified in Fig. 5.3 but also encompasses potential productivity gains due to reduced government market intervention (Kuźnar, 2004) and improvements to developing nations' competitiveness in agricultural markets due to reduced farming subsidies in rich countries (Morkis, 1995; Puślecki, 2013; Hajdukiewicz, 2016). Arguments are also made that a trade deal may provide an external source of motivation to implement necessary structural reforms that enhance domestic markets' efficiency. The FTAs are also perceived as a chance to improve the country's security by building trust among trading nations, facilitating international political cooperation, and diversifying import and export markets. For example, CEFTA was designed by the Central European countries, including Poland, as a vehicle for joining the European Union. Through its provisions, the agreement enabled the economic and political integration among the region's nations and the EU (Pera, 2003; Molendowski & Klimczak,

2015). A couple of post-2008 articles include ease of cross-border profit transfers and favouring the growth of multinational corporations as opportunities associated with trade deals (Liberska, 2010; Dąbkowski, 2016). However, it has to be noted that both authors also warn of possible negative consequences of such solutions if not adequately controlled.

As previously mentioned, Polish trade literature tends to have a favourable attitude towards trade deals. Thus, it is not surprising that the list of expected costs of FTAs is shorter than the list of benefits and that, when looking at the top of Fig. 5.3, we count six benefits which are more frequently mentioned than the most frequently appearing cost. According to our sample articles, the majority of the costs of signing a trade deal relate to the sacrifice of control over regulations and standards and allowing lower quality goods into the domestic market. The most frequently raised costs are reduced food safety and standards. This particular issue is debated mostly in the post-2008 publications in which authors fear the adverse impacts of opening the EU agricultural and food markets to imports from the US and Canada. They worry that many EU farmers and food producers will be unable to compete against the much larger scale farms from across the Atlantic and that the more lax food safety regulations on the American continent will enable the importers to undercut the prices of food produced within the EU. This may lead to large-scale collapses of domestic food producers, expose the EU to external shocks, and weaken its food security (e.g. Oręziak, 2015; Gostomski & Michałowski, 2016; Krzyżanowski, 2016). These worries are also reflected in the list of threats. Numerous authors perceive the imports of GMO food and hormone-fed animals as a potential threat to Europeans' health and a threat to more traditional methods of food production (e.g. Kaliszuk, 2016; Gostomski & Michałowski, 2016; Korzycka & Wojciechowski, 2017; Załucki, 2017). This links to deterioration of consumer rights as potentially less healthy products could crowd out healthier goods, thereby restricting household choices (e.g. Oręziak, 2015). Some worry that FTAs provisions on food labelling, in particular obscuring the content of GMO or hormone-fed meat in products, could limit consumers' ability to make informed choices about their consumption (e.g. Kaliszuk, 2016; Korzycka & Wojciechowski, 2017).

Another oft-indicated cost of signing a trade deal is allowing foreign competition into domestic markets which may put domestic producers in an unfavourable situation (e.g. Gruchelski & Niemczyk, 2004; Skrzypczyńska, 2012). This may have knock-on consequences for employment in affected sectors and lead to deteriorated work conditions as domestic employers cut costs to increase their efficiency and competitiveness (e.g. Hajdukiewicz, 2002; Marszk, 2010). Some authors noted that a very likely cost of an agreement with the US would be serious legal limitations for government interventions in domestic markets, including the provision of public services such as healthcare (e.g. Nacewska-Twardowska, 2017; Załucki, 2017). All these put together suggest that trade deals may entail considerable structural adjustment costs.

The articles in our sample indicate several other threats that could potentially harm signatories of FTAs in certain conditions. Broadly speaking, since the debates on TTIP and CETA, the discussion has circled around the balance of power between governments and corporations, and free markets and social provision. Some authors worry that modern trade deals risk giving too much power to multinational corporations and weaken the position of sovereign governments (e.g. Marszk, 2010; Zajaczkowski, 2014). This may be exemplified by inadequate dispute resolution arrangements which enshroud trade disputes in secrecy (e.g. Zając, 2008; Grącik-Zajaczkowski, 2014), negotiation of trade deals behind closed doors but with the participation of corporate lobbyists that may undermine the democratic process (e.g. Kaplan, 2002; Gostomski & Michałowski, 2016) and trust in governments by opening it to accusations of serving particular foreign or corporate interests (e.g. Wróbel, 2014; Kaliszuk, 2016), leading to the marketisation of public services (e.g. Oręziak, 2015; Załucki, 2017).

Finally, too far-going liberalisation of markets is also seen as a threat to living standards. The uncontrolled pursuit of narrowly defined economic efficiency and drive to boosting international competitiveness are seen to threaten the environmental conditions and standards and risk raising economic and social inequalities (e.g. Liberska, 2010; Michalska-Haduch, 2012). Imports from low-wage countries may undermine the sustainability of domestic production while the free flow of goods and capital may encourage firms to move their production to other, cheaper countries (e.g. Hajdukiewicz, 2002; Błaszczuk-Zawiła, 2012). In both cases leading to job losses and possibly triggering the "race to the bottom" whereby countries cut their regulations, standards, and taxes to maintain international competitiveness at the expense of the living standards of large pockets of the population. Conversely, low-wage countries may see higher demand for their exports, which may raise their domestic prices of certain products, making them unaffordable for the local poor (e.g. Morkis,

1995; Pera, 2016). Although many of the analysed publications notice potentially harmful consequences of the FTAs, the absence of discussion or proposals on how to avoid or remedy the negative outcomes and redistribute gains from trade is striking.

Of course, such simple comparisons may provide an inaccurate picture of the expert sentiment as they do not take into consideration the relative weights of the presented factors. It is not difficult to imagine a situation in which a single cost or threat outweighs several smaller benefits. For example, a risk of losing control over domestic markets or a collapse of an industry which employs vast pockets of society may outweigh benefits of a newly gained access to a foreign market such as the creation of new jobs in other, marginal sectors, standardisation of trade rules or access to imports which enhance consumer choice. Another obstacle to presenting a weighted synthesis of the expert sentiment is the scarcity of quantitative evaluations of the effects of the FTAs in the Polish literature, which was noted in the previous section. Since in most cases no estimates of even the most basic consequences are provided, it is impossible to perform a meta-analysis which would objectively quantify and summarise the literature's dominant attitude. In defence of the authors in our sample, some aspects may be difficult to quantify, for example it is very difficult to assign a monetary value to the deterioration of democracy. These shortcomings limit our analysis of expert sentiment to the simple counts like those mentioned above and counting the frequency with which individual benefits, costs, threats, and opportunities are mentioned in the literature, as displayed in Fig. 5.3. In the following section, we build an "expert knowledge dictionary" which will be used in Chap. 6 to measure the degree to which the expert debate feeds into the more popular online discussions.

5.4 Expert Knowledge Dictionary

Our Expert Knowledge Dictionary is a set of professional vocabulary frequently encountered in the Polish FTA literature. The words and phrases included in such a dictionary are expected to signal that the text is based on expert knowledge, which is based on research and experience in the fields of international trade and economics. Such knowledge can be either declarative or procedural and is organised into methodological structures or schemas that enable its holders to categorise and construct a mental representation of a specific problem and store and communicate information in a specific domain of exploration (Nokes et al. 2010). The need to store and communicate knowledge results in a formation of vocabulary or jargon that is discipline-specific and is a fundamental building block of the "code" that experts in a given discipline use to communicate with each other and, to a lesser degree, with external and non-expert audiences.

In Chap. 6 we work under an assumption that the appearance of the expert phrases and words in the public discussion is an indicator that it is grounded in or informed by expert knowledge. Nonetheless, we expect the debate in popular media to use language and terms easily understood by non-expert audiences and only occasionally include (and explain) terms that are characteristic of an advanced debate among subject experts. Therefore, when constructing our Expert Knowledge Dictionary, we go beyond a narrowly defined set of words indicative of an advanced expert understanding of international trade. We also include words and terms that frequently appear in the analysed academic literature, whose use is not necessarily restricted only to economics or international trade and are likely to appear in a merit-based discussion among non-experts. In practice, this means the inclusion of such terms as *Single Market*, *domestic market*, *global market*, *bilateral agreement*, *preferential trade agreement*, *employment*, *genetically modified organisms* (*GMO*), and so on.[8]

To form our Expert Knowledge Dictionary, we focus on the corpus, or body, of text from the sample of 51 research articles discussed in the previous sections. Our analysis follows the mixed methods methodological approach (Teddlie and Tashakkori 2003) and takes advantage of the recent advances in the computational linguistics resources for the Polish language, in particular, the lexicometric tools made available by the Common Language Resources and Technology Infrastructure (CLARIN-PL).[9] The multi-stage process of categorisation and re-categorisation of FTA-related

[8] The corresponding Polish terms encountered in the body of text are: *Jednolity Rynek*, *rynek krajowy*, *rynek globalny*, *umowa dwustronna*, *preferencyjna umowa handlowa* and *zatrudnienie*, *organizmy zmodyfikowane genetycznie (GMO)*.

[9] CLARIN-PL (https://clarin-pl.eu/) is a section of the pan-European research project aiming at creation and development of electronic language tools and resources for natural language processing, aiding researchers in humanities and social sciences in the analysis of large collections of texts in Polish.

expert terms relies on frequency analysis, phrase retrieval, and co-occurrence analysis.

Before describing step-by-step the procedure applied to build the expert dictionary, we should make some methodological remarks. The high degree of complexity of Polish grammar (Wawer 2012) and relative heterogeneity of the analysed sample (the articles come from several research disciplines) render a fully inductive approach that would be free of a priori refinement of text, such as unsupervised machine learning, inappropriate (Fersini 2017; Pawar et al. 2016). Instead, we resort to a semi-inductive method based on keyword categorisation models to create the Expert Knowledge Dictionary. The chosen approach is grounded in the classical content analysis methods (e.g. Krippendorff 2019; Bauer 2000) and the interpretative paradigm (e.g. Kobylarek 2014; Angen 2000; Fensel 1992). In practice, this means that researchers consider only individual textual units, such as words and phrases, based on the frequency of their occurrence and co-occurrence in the analysed text. The element of the researchers' interpretation or judgement has potential implications for the objectivity of the used classification method. To alleviate the risks associated with the decision's subjectivity, which words and phrases should be included in the dictionary, the candidate terms were independently reviewed and then discussed by three researchers.

Furthermore, since the analysis was performed on contextless words and phrases (i.e. not considered in the context of an entire document, paragraph, or sentence), whenever the classification appeared problematic, the researchers considered the context of the occurrence of a particular term. We supplemented this process by the use of tools designed specifically for the Polish language to extract word collocations and proper names appearing in the analysed body of text, as described below. Thus, the dictionary creation process was iterative and consisted of a sequence of the coding and re-coding procedures that, with each step, were aimed at refining the final outcome. This sequence of steps is illustrated in Fig. 5.4 and described in the remainder of this section.

As shown in Fig. 5.4, the starting point of our analysis is the corpus of the text contained in the sample of 51 research publications. First, we retrieve single words and phrases (or n-grams) consisting of two or more words which meet the following criteria:

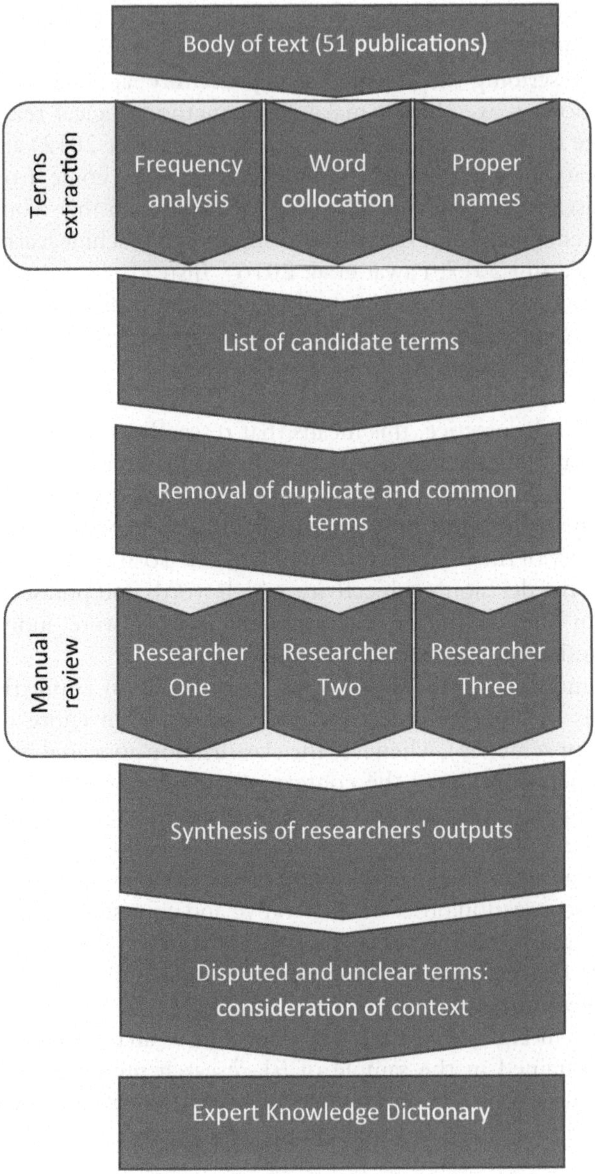

Fig. 5.4 Construction process of the Expert Knowledge Dictionary

a. words occurring at least ten times and phrases appearing at least three times in the entire sample of 51 articles covering the years from 1994 to 2019,[10]
b. words occurring at least ten times and phrases appearing at least three times in the articles published in years 2008 to 2019 (73% of the sample),
c. words occurring at least five times and phrases appearing at least twice in the articles published between 1994 and 2008 (27% of the sample).

We apply different criteria to the two sub-periods because, as argued previously, the literature's focus was not necessarily the same in the 1990s and early 2000s as in the 2010s. Thus, given the much smaller number of articles published until 2008, we would risk losing expert terms related to issues and concepts that played a central role in the early years of our sample but were not extensively discussed in the subsequent period.

To extract words and phrases meeting the above criteria we use three lexicometric resources. The key tool used in the process is TermoPL developed for automatic extraction of Polish terminology.[11] Since the tool is created specifically for Polish language, it is capable of retrieving noun phrases and term candidates, recognising nested terms, and unifying terms' morphological variants (Marciniak et al. 2016). We supplement the frequency analysis by performing simple word and phrase counts using two alternative pieces of software: AntConc for words and phrases and NVivo for words.[12] Both of them identify the frequency with which terms appear in the text, but not being specifically developed for the Polish language, they are unable to perform any contextual or morphological analysis. The use of these multiple and independent tools serve as a quality

[10] The selection of ten and three for the threshold may appear somewhat subjective. To ensure that we do not lose valid observations by applying these restrictions, we also consider a sub-sample of words and phrases appearing eight and two times, respectively, in the entire corpus of text. We conclude that the loss of terms is insignificant. In general, our threshold values are consistent with those applied in Działo et al. (2017), and Gawronska-Nowak et al. (2019), whose analyses were conducted on considerably smaller corpora of text.

[11] More information about TermoPL and its source code can be found at http://zil.ipipan.waw.pl/TermoPL and https://ws.clarin-pl.eu/termopl.shtml.

[12] NVivo is commercial software package commonly used for qualitative data analysis. AntConc is a freeware corpus analysis toolkit for concordancing and text analysis, developed by Laurence Anthony and available at https://www.laurenceanthony.net/software/antconc/.

check to ensure that we do not miss any relevant terms or phrases in our analysis.

We also take advantage of two more services developed specifically for the Polish language and made available by CLARIN-PL. MeWeX is a tool designed to extract word collocations from a body of text and construct a dictionary of multi-word lexical terms.[13] Thus, it allows us to identify repeating terms that consist of more than one word, for example *foreign direct investment* (Polish: *bezpośrednie inwestycje zagraniczne*). The other tool, NER, has been developed to identify proper names within a body of text.[14] It enables us to extract, among others, titles of trade-related agreements, legal documents, mechanisms, bodies, and institutions which may serve as a signal of expert knowledge, for example *Agreement on the Application of Sanitary and Phytosanitary Measures*, *Dispute Settlement Body*, and *Technical Assistance Information Exchange Office*.

In the next step, the outputs from each of the five tools are merged and "cleaned". We remove duplicate terms as well as common words and phrases which without a doubt frequently appear in non-expert debates, for example the *Polish government*, the *United States*, *period*, *creation*, or *growth*.[15] We also apply stemming and lemmatisation to reduce the inflectional forms of the same words and phrases. This way we achieve the first, crude version of our expert dictionary which consists of terms encountered mostly, but not only, in the macroeconomics, international trade and finance literature, along with the names and titles of trade agreements, institutions, trade policy tools, macroeconomic variables, theoretical economic models, as well as terms characteristic for the key trade sectors and industries.

Subsequently, the dictionary is independently reviewed by three separate researchers who mark each term as (i) *definitely expert and to be kept*, (ii) *definitely irrelevant and to be removed*, or (iii) *requiring further investigation*. The researchers' categorisations are then compared. Terms which are unanimously categorised as belonging to the first or second category

[13] MeWeX is available at https://ws.clarin-pl.eu/mewex.shtml.

[14] NER is available at http://ws.clarin-pl.eu/ner.shtml.

[15] Note that some words do not signal expert knowledge within a particular discipline or informed debate on a particular issue when used on their own. For example, it is impossible to unequivocally link the words *creation* and *growth* to the expert trade debate as they can be used in many contexts, disciplines, as well as "lay" conversations. However, when used in conjunction with other words they form terms which clearly belong to the international trade's expert vocabulary, for example *trade creation* and *export-led growth*.

are actioned accordingly. Terms belonging to the third category and those on which the reviewers did not reach a unanimous judgement are analysed within the contexts they appear in the initial body of text. They are included in the expert dictionary if, following a discussion among the three researchers, at least two of them perceive them as representing expert or professional vocabulary.

Following the above process, we arrive at the final version of the Expert Knowledge Dictionary, which lists 1540 terms. As shown in Fig. 5.5, single words account for just under a quarter of the dictionary (360 terms), and the remainder consists of multi-word phrases (1180 terms), of which two-word phrases represent the vast majority. The longer terms, consisting of five or more words, tend to represent names and titles of international agreements and agencies. The examples include *General Agreement on Tariffs and Trade*, *United Nations Conference on Trade and Development*, and *WTO Program for National Self-Assessments of Trade Facilitation Needs and Priorities*, which at 11 words long is the longest term in our dictionary. Examples of the most frequently appearing terms are displayed

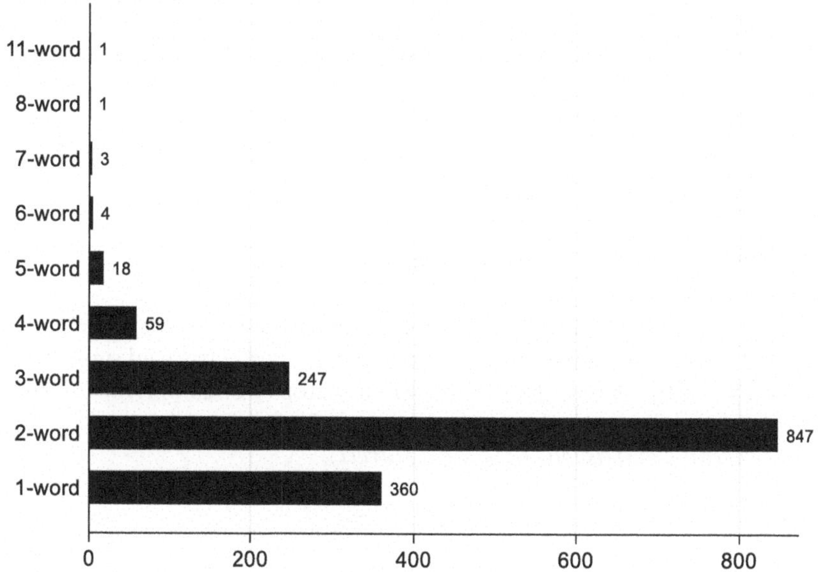

Fig. 5.5 Number of terms by length

Single words	Phrases	Proper names
agriculture *(rolnictwo)*	dispute resolution *(rozstrzyganie sporów)*	ERM 2 *(ERM 2)*
cooperation *(współpraca)*	duty tariff *(stawka celna)*	European Commission *(Komisja Europejska)*
custom duty *(cło)*	economic growth *(wzrost gospodarczy)*	European Union Single Market *(Jednolity Rynek Unii Europejskiej)*
development *(rozwój)*	free trade *(wolny handel)*	GATT-General Agreement on Tariffs and Trade *(GATT-Ogólny Układ w sprawie Taryf Celnych i Handlu)*
export *(eksport)*	free trade zone *(strefa wolnego handlu)*	Information Technojogy Agreement *(Porozumienie Informatyczne)*
GDP *(PKB)*	intellectual property *(własność intelektualna)*	Technical Assistance Information Exchange Office
GMO *(GMO)*	member state *(państwo członkowskie)*	UN Conference on Trade and Development *(Konferencja NZ ds. Handlu i Rozwoju)*
import *(import)*	trade creation effect *(efekt kreacji handlu)*	World Bank *(Bank Światowy)*
investment *(inwestycja)*	trade liberalisation *(liberalizacja handlu)*	World Custom Organization *(Światowa Organizacja Celna)*
market *(rynek)*	trade policy *(polityka handlowa)*	World Trade Organisation *(Światowa Organizacja Handlu)*

Fig. 5.6 Examples of the most frequent terms (Polish language in parentheses)

in Fig. 5.6. They seem to confirm the observations made in the previous section that the debate in the Polish research literature has paid significant attention to the issues of the agricultural sector (words: *agriculture* and *GMO*) and the membership of the European Union (proper names: *ERM 2*, *European Commission*, *EU Single Market*).

5.5 Summarising Remarks

The purpose of this chapter was to present a picture of the Polish-language academic literature on the FTAs. We used some basic metrics to compare its prolificity to the literature in English, German, French, and Italian. This way we showed that the Polish research publications followed patterns broadly similar to those of the discourse in the other four languages, albeit at a much smaller scale when compared to the volume of outputs in English. The correlation analysis in Sect. 5.1 led us to a weak proposition that, judging by the magnitude and dynamics of academic publications, our study might be representative of the broader expert discourse on the FTA issues in the non-English, European academic literature. We, then, focused on the content of the Polish literature and presented some of the key and dominating themes and sentiments. Based on a sample of approximately a quarter of all academic articles published in Polish between 1995 and 2019, we noted that the sentiment of the majority of outputs was unequivocally favourable towards free trade and only one in seven articles was sceptical or openly negative in the evaluation of the impacts of the discussed FTAs. We also noted that, when compared to the mainstream trade literature in English, the Polish research outputs appeared to be much more qualitative and descriptive, often limited to plain reporting on developments in trade negotiations or summarising contents of official FTA-related documents, and very seldom adopted a quantitative approach.

However, the most important purpose of this chapter was to lay the ground for Chap. 6 by constructing the "Expert Knowledge Dictionary" which will be used to conduct the content analysis of the Polish internet news sources and examine the degree to which they link to the expert debate and rely on the expert knowledge. Thus, we prepared a set of 1540 terms frequently encountered in the Polish FTA literature and which are likely to appear in any merit-based discussion on FTAs among non-experts

Appendix

The list of Polish-language research articles included in the sample analysed in this chapter.

1. Ambroziak, Ł. (2016). Efekt kreacji w handlu Polski z Kanadą po wejściu w życie umowy CETA. *Unia Europejska.Pl*, *2*(237), 19–28.
2. Błaszczuk-Zawiła, M. (2012). Skutki przystąpienia Rosji do WTO dla stosunków UE-Rosja. *Unia Europejska.Pl*, *4*(215), 7–17.

3. Czarny, E., Folfas, P., & Menkes, J. (2017). Transatlantyckie partnerstwo w dziedzinie handlu i inwestycji (TTIP) a system bezpieczeństwa regionalnego i globalnego. *Studia Oeconomica Posnaniensia*, *5*(8), 114–126. https://doi.org/10.18559/soep.2017.8.8
4. Czubek, H. (2006). Analiza dynamiki struktury towarowej polskiego handlu zagranicznego z Unią Europejską i CEFTA. *Zeszyty Naukowe Uniwersytetu Ekonomicznego w Krakowie*, (723), 29–44.
5. Dąbkowski, A. (2016). Międzynarodowe traktaty wolnego handlu – NAFTA, TTIP, ASEAN. *Zeszyty Naukowe Uczelni Vistula*, *48*(3), 52–68.
6. Dugiel, W. (2017). WTO po 10. Konferencji Ministerialnej w Nairobi – koniec liberalizacji wielostronnej? *Horyzonty Polityki*, *8*(22), 11–30. https://doi.org/10.17399/HP.2017.082201
7. Dunin-Wąsowicz, M. (2015). Kwestia walutowa a TTIP w perspektywie międzynarodowej ekonomii politycznej . *Stosunki Międzynarodowe*, *2*(51), 167–187. 16. https://doi.org/10.7366/020909612201508
8. Dunin-Wąsowicz, M. (2014). Umowa TTIP a kwestia walutowa. *Unia Europejska.Pl*, *3*(226), 6–15.
9. Gostomski, E., & Michałowski, T. (2016). Szanse i zagrożenia związane z zawarciem kompleksowej umowy gospodarczo-handlowej (CETA) między Unią Europejską i Kanadą. *Pieniądze i Więź*, *4*(73), 69–76.
10. Grącik-Zajaczkowski, M. (2014). Spory handlowe Unii Europejskiej i USA w ramach WTO. *Krakowskie Studia Międzynarodowe*, *9*(2), 59–76. https://doi.org/10.4135/9781412939607.n768
11. Gruchelski, M., & Niemczyk, J. (2004). Najnowsze porozumienie rolne w światowej organizacji handlu (WTO)-implikacje dla Polski. *Postępy Techniki Przetwórstwa Spożywczego*, *14*, 76–80.
12. Hajdukiewicz, A. (2017). Kierunki zmian Wspólnej Polityki Rolnej Unii Europejskiej w kontekście negocjacji handlowych na forum WTO i Brexitu. *Horyzonty Polityki*, *8*(22), 109–130. https://doi.org/10.17399/HP.2017.082206
13. Hajdukiewicz, A. (2016). Od Bali do Nairobi – nowy impuls dla wielostronnej liberalizacji handlu rolnegona forum WTO. *Biznes Międzynarodowy w Gospodarce Globalnej*, *35*(1), 209–221. https://doi.org/10.4467/23539496IB.16.016.5597

14. Hajdukiewicz, A. (2002). Możliwości rozwoju światowego handlu w świetle oceny funkcjonowania wielostronnego systemu handlowego GATT/WTO. *Zeszyty Naukowe Uniwersytetu Ekonomicznego w Krakowie*, (601), 7–17.
15. Kaliszuk, E. (2016). Postanowienia umowy CETA w sferze biotechnologii rolniczej–wnioski dla rokowań umowy TTIP. *Unia Europejska.Pl*, *1*(236), 17–22.
16. Kaplan, D. M. (2002). GMO, WTO i bezpieczeństwo żywności. *Człowiek w Kulturze*, *14*(2002), 157–165. https://doi.org/10.1017/CBO9781107415324.004
17. Korzycka, M., & Wojciechowski, P. (2017). Regulacja prawna żywności genetycznie zmodyfikowanej w USA i UE w kontekście planowanego Transatlantyckiego Porozumienia Handlowo-Inwestycyjnego (TTIP). *Studia Iuridica Lublinensia*, *26*(1), 465–488. https://doi.org/10.17951/sil.2017.26.1.465
18. Kowalik, P. (2015). Ocena poziomu rozwoju gospodarczego i powiązań z zagranicą krajów na przykładzie członków NAFTA. *Ekonometria*, *2*(48), 114–125. https://doi.org/10.15611/ekt.2015.2.10
19. Kowalik, P. (2008). NAFTA – 12 lat funkcjonowania. *Ekonomia i Międzynarodowe Stosunki Gospodarcze*, *18*(12), 109–124.
20. Kruszka, M. (2001). Międzynarodowy handel usługami w świetle zasad WTO. *Ekonomia*, (3), 120–134.
21. Krzyżanowski, J. (2016). Szanse i zagrożenia dla rolnictwa i konsumentów żywności w krajach Unii Europejskiej wynikające z ewentualnego porozumienia TTIP. *Zagadnienia Ekonomiki Rolnej*, *348*(3), 3–23. https://doi.org/10.5604/00441600.1218192
22. Kuźnar, A. (2004). Proces liberalizacji międzynarodowego handlu uslugami w ramach WTO oraz jego skutki. *International Journal of Management and Economics*, *15*, 134–159.
23. Liberska, B. (2010). Integracja krajów NAFTA a globalny kryzys gospodarczy. *Ameryka Łacińska. Kwartalnik Analityczno-Informacyjny*, 37–48.
24. Ludwikowski, R. R. (2019). Strategie handlowe Donalda Trumpa. Kilka refleksji nad procesem transformacji NAFTA w USMCA. *Krakowskie Studia Międzynarodowe*, *4*(XVI), 213–222. https://doi.org/10.34697/2451-0610-ksm-2019-4-014

25. Majchrowska, E. (2015). TTIP a WTO: szansa czy zagrożenie? *Krakowskie Studia Międzynarodowe*, *12*(4), 149–164.
26. Majchrowska, E. (2017). Perspektywy rozwoju stosunków handlowych Polski z Kanadą w świetle umowy CETA. *Prace Naukowe Uniwersytetu Ekonomicznego we Wrocławiu*, (498), 181–191. https://doi.org/10.15611/pn.2017.498.17
27. Marszk, A. (2010). Północnoamerykańskie Porozumienie o Wolnym Handlu (NAFTA) i jego postanowienia dotyczące bezpośrednich inwestycji zagranicznych. *Ekonomia Międzynarodowa*, *2010*(1), 66–85.
28. Michalska-Haduch, A. (2012). Efekt kreacji handlu w wymianie handlowej Meksyku z krajami partnerskimi po wejściu w życie porozumienia NAFTA. *International Journal of Management and Economics*, *33*, 116–143.
29. Miklaszewski, S. (2005). Próba bilansu dokonań i przyszłość CEFTA w świetle rozszerzenia Unii Europejskiej. *Zeszyty Naukowe Uniwersytetu Ekonomicznego w Krakowie*, (695), 5–21.
30. Molendowski, E. (2006). Proces tworzenia strefy wolnego handlu w ramach środkowoeuropejskiej umowy o wolnym handlu (CEFTA) – najważniejsze skutki dla Polski. *Zeszyty Naukowe Uniwersytetu Ekonomicznego w Krakowie*, (721), 67–84.
31. Molendowski, E. (2005). Handel wewnątrzgałęziowy krajów CEFTA z państwami Unii Europejskiej-podstawowe tendencje w latach 1992-2002. *Zeszyty Naukowe Uniwersytetu Ekonomicznego w Krakowie*, (695), 41–59.
32. Molendowski, E., & Klimczak, Ł. (2015). Porozumienie CEFTA-2006 – jego znaczenie dla rozwoju handlu wzajemnego krajów Bałkanów Zachodnich. *Prace Naukowe Uniwersytetu Ekonomicznego we Wrocławiu*, (407), 39–50. https://doi.org/10.15611/pn.2015.407.03
33. Morkis, G. (1995). Układ Europejski i akt końcowy Rundy Urugwajskiej GATT a polski rynek artykułów rolno-spożywczych. *Żywność. Technologia. Jakość.*, *3*(4), 32–39.
34. Nacewska-Twardowska, A. (2017). Prognoza zmian w eksporcie państw członkowskich Unii Europejskiej do Stanów Zjednoczonych w kontekście TTIP. *Prace Naukowe Uniwersytetu Ekonomicznego we Wrocławiu*, (466), 167–177. https://doi.org/10.15611/pn.2017.466.17

35. Olkuski, T., Sikora, A. P., Sikora, M. P., Szurlej, A., & Tora, B. (2016). Rynek gazu ziemnego w kontekście umowy TTIP. *Rynek Energii*, *5*, 16–21.
36. Oręziak, L. (2015). TTIP – Transatlantyckie Partnerstwo w sprawie Handlu i Inwestycji – źródłem zagrożeń dla gospodarki i społeczeństwa. *Studia z Polityki Publicznej*, *4*(8), 81–106. https://doi.org/10.33119/kszpp.2015.4.5
37. Pera, J. (2003). Perspektywy kształtowania się współpracy subregionalnej krajów CEFTA w kontekście integracji z Unią Europejską. *Zeszyty Naukowe Uniwersytetu Ekonomicznego w Krakowie*, (634), 105–124.
38. Pera, J. (2016). Bilans ryzyka TTIP w zakresie liberalizacji handlu produktami rolno-spożywczymi w modelu CGEM–GTAP. *Ekonomia XXI Wieku*, *3*(11), 141–157. https://doi.org/10.15611/e21.2016.3.12
39. Poczta-Wajda, A. (2010). Znaczenie WTO w dynamizowaniu procesu liberalizacji handlu artykułami rolno-żywnościowymi. *Roczniki Naukowe Stowarzyszenia Ekonomistów Rolnictwa i Agrobiznesu*, *4*(12), 275–280.
40. Puślecki, Z. W. (2013). Wokół osłabiania neoprotekcjonizmu rolnego Unii Europejskiej w ramach i poza WTO. *Ekonomia*, *2*(23), 30–48.
41. Ronek, G. (2007). Światowa Organizacja Handlu (WTO) na początku XXI wieku. *Studia Politologiczne*, 73–82.
42. Rostowska, M. (2013). GMO, hormony i inne kontrowersje: kwestia rolnictwa w negocjacjach nad TTIP. *Biuletyn Polskiego Instytutu Spraw Międzynarodowych*, *108*(1084), 1–2.
43. Sikora, A. P., Jarosz, R., Sikora, M. P., Szurlej, A., & Cios, S. (2016). Analiza kosztów i korzyści polski i ue związanych z planowaną umową handlową między UE i USA (TTIP). *Przemysl Chemiczny*, *95*(5), 883–889. https://doi.org/10.15199/62.2016.5.1
44. Skrzypczyńska, J. (2012). Polska w GATT/WTO. *Przegląd Politologiczny*, (1), 83–91. https://doi.org/10.14746/pp.2012.17.1.6
45. Wróbel, A. (2014). Funkcjonalność i dysfunkcjonalność wielostronnego systemu handlowego WTO. *Współczesne Problemy Ekonomiczne - Zeszyty Naukowe Uniwersytetu Szczecińskiego*, *8*(800), 99–107.

46. Zając, M. (2008). Rozwój stosunków handlowych i współpracy gospodarczej pomiędzy UE a NAFTA na przykładzie USA. *Zeszyty Naukowe Uniwersytetu Ekonomicznego w Krakowie*, (787), 115–133.
47. Zajaczkowski, M. (2018). Runda z Dohy WTO–próba przyjęcia reguł sprzyjających interesom krajów rozwijających się. *Studia Ekonomiczne*, (372), 205–219.
48. Zajaczkowski, M. (2014). Sekwencyjność rozwoju stosunków GATT/WTO z krajami rozwijającymi się. *Kwartalnik Kolegium Ekonomiczno-Społecznego „Studia i Prace"*, *20*(4), 33–57.
49. Załucki, K. (2017). TTIP – szansa czy zagrożenie dla Unii Europejskiej, jej przedsiębiorców i obywateli? Próba analizy skutków umowy. *Zeszyty Naukowe Politechniki Śląskiej. Seria: Organizacja i Zarządzanie*, *1981*(106), 45–55. https://doi.org/10.29119/1641-3466.2017.106.4
50. Żołądkiewicz, K. (2017). Porozumienie transpacyficzne (TPP) bez Stanów Zjednoczonych. *Studia i Prace WNEiZ US*, *49*(2), 105–115. https://doi.org/10.18276/sip.2017.49/2-08
51. Żołądkiewicz, K. (2015). Partnerstwo Transpacyficzne (TPP) jako nowe porozumienie integracyjne w regionie Azji-Pacyfiku. *Studia i Prace WNEiZ US*, *41*(1), 93–110.

References

Angen, M. J. (2000). Evaluating interpretive inquiry: Reviewing the validity debate and opening the dialogue. Qualitative Health Research, 10, 378-395.

Bauer, M. (2000). Classical content analysis: a review. In Bauer, M. W., & Gaskell, G. Qualitative researching with text, image and sound (pp. 132-151). London: SAGE Publications Ltd.

Działo, J., Gawrońska-Nowak, B., & Jura, J. (2017). Social debate on free trade agreements: Illusions versus reality. Economics and Sociology, 10(3), 116–135.

Fensel D. (1992) Knowledge acquisition and the interpretative paradigm. In: Schmalhofer F., Strube G., Wetter T. (eds) Contemporary Knowledge Engineering and Cognition. Lecture Notes in Computer Science, vol 622. Springer, Berlin, Heidelberg.

Fersini, E. (2017). Sentiment Analysis in Social Networks: a Machine Learning Perspective. In: F. Pozzi, E. Fersini, E. Messina and Bing Liu (eds). Sentiment Analysis in Social Networks. Elsevier, 91-111.

Gawronska-Nowak, B., Beck, K., & Valdivieso, P. (2019). Expert knowledge status quo in the internet provided public debate on free trade agreements. Meta-analysis of Polish literature. Economics and Sociology, 12(1), 248–261.

Kobylarek, Aleksander (2014). Text analysis in the interpretative paradigm of research. Qualitative Content Analysis in Research Conducted in Cyberspace, 25.

Krippendorff, Klaus (2019). Content analysis: An introduction to its methodology. 4th ed. Sage Publications.

Marciniak, M., Mykowiecka, A., & Rychlik, P. (2016, May). TermoPL – a flexible tool for terminology extraction. In Proceedings of the Tenth International Conference on Language Resources and Evaluation (LREC'16) (pp. 2278-2284).

Nokes, T.J., C.D. Schunn, M.T.H. Chi, 2010. Problem Solving and Human Expertise, editor(s): Penelope Peterson, Eva Baker, Barry McGaw, International Encyclopedia of Education (Third Edition), Elsevier, pages 265-272

Pawar, A. B., Jawale, M. A., Kyatanavar, D. N. (2016). Fundamentals of Sentiment Analysis: Concepts and Methodology. In: Pedrycz, W., Chen, SM. (eds). Sentiment Analysis and Ontology Engineering. Studies in Computational Intelligence, 639. Springer, Cham.

Teddlie, C., & Tashakkori, A. (2003), Major issues and controversies in the use of mixed methods in the social and behavioral sciences. In: C. Tashakkori & A. Teddlie (Eds.), Handbook of mixed methods in social and behavioral research, Thousand Oaks, CA: Sage, pp. 3-50.

Wawer, A. (2012). Extracting emotive patterns for languages with rich morphology. International Journal of Computational Linguistics and Applications, 3, 11-24.

CHAPTER 6

Online Free Trade Discourse: Expert Knowledge and Attitudes

Abstract We conduct a study of the public debate on Free Trade Agreements by analysing news articles and readers' comments published in the Polish online media between 1996 and 2019. Working on a large sample of online articles and readers' posts, we conduct content analysis of seven Polish internet news outlets and investigate how much expert knowledge is contained in the news articles written by journalists as well as accompanying comments posted by readers. We also investigate how the demand and supply of the news on international trade in Poland compare to those in other European countries. The analysis considers the economic narratives surrounding the free trade debate in popular media. For that purpose, we scrutinise the co-occurrence and frequency of mentions of individual FTAs in the media as well as explore the broader economic and political context in which trade deals are discussed.

Keywords Expert knowledge • Online media • Content analysis • Economic narratives • FTA narratives • Co-occurrence analysis

The costs and benefits of FTAs remain a hotly debated topic of ongoing academic and political discourses. They also attract the attention of the general public who typically draw their information from news services, newspapers, and popular magazines. As with many issues, journalists working for these outlets are responsible for informing society and,

B. Gawrońska-Nowak et al., *Trade Wins or Trade Wars*,
https://doi.org/10.1007/978-3-030-76997-0_6

consequently, the quality of the passed information which then forms the basis of the public opinion on the free trade issues. Nonetheless, professional journalists no longer have a monopoly on informing the general public. The advent of widespread internet and social media has democratised this debate and enabled laypersons to join in and broadcast their news, views, and other information to large audiences. The ability to immediately share information, more or less factual, means that the internet and social media have become freely available outlets for a variety of views, misconceptions, and stereotypes which may promote either positive or harmful attitudes within the wider society. The shortness of social media posts strips the debate of its complexity, meaning that more nuanced key arguments are often ignored and authors of misleading messages do not need to provide supporting evidence or explain their views in detail. Unlike expert debates, the views shared by non-expert users on the internet may be based on truths, half-truths, and fake news, leading to a variety of positive and negative attitudes among users. It would be naïve to ignore the role and importance of those emotions in any successful implementation of major international treaties such as Free Trade Agreements.

In this chapter, we conduct a study of the public debate on Free Trade Agreements by analysing news articles and readers' comments published in the Polish online media between 1996 and 2019. The main aim is to investigate to what extent this debate is informed by expert knowledge and in Chap. 7 we investigate how it correlates with attitudes and emotions towards FTAs conveyed by journalists and readers. We focus our attention on online news portals which are the most popular source of information for nearly 61% of adult Poles. Their popularity by far outstrips all other sources: the second most popular is social media, such as Facebook and Twitter, which is indicated by 38% of respondents as a key source of information (IBIMS, 2021). Working on a large sample of online articles and readers' posts, we conduct content analysis of seven Polish internet news outlets and investigate how much expert knowledge is contained in the news articles written by journalists as well as accompanying comments posted by readers. We focus on the same seven trade agreements as in the previous chapters: CEFTA, CETA, GATT, NAFTA, TTIP, TPP, and WTO.

The chapter is divided into three main areas of exploration. First, we present and discuss our data sample and investigate how the demand and supply of the news on international trade in Poland compare to those in other European countries. Second, we consider the economic narratives surrounding the free trade debate in popular media. In doing so, we follow the example of Robert Shiller (2019) and scrutinise the frequency of mentions of individual FTAs in the media as well as explore the broader economic and political context in which trade deals are discussed. We also perform a co-occurrence analysis that lets us detect which FTAs are closely related in the public view and are often debated in conjunction. In the third area of exploration, we use the Expert Knowledge Dictionary developed in Chap. 5 to determine how much expert knowledge is conveyed in online news articles and readers' comments posted below them. We then use all these results in the next chapter (Chap. 7) where we confront the sentiment (attitudes) and emotions towards free trade expressed by both journalists and readers, and we check how they relate to the content of expert knowledge.

Throughout this chapter, we interchangeably use various terms to refer to articles posted on the analysed texts. Whenever we say online articles, news articles, internet portals, journalists' texts, we mean content written or published online by journalists, editorial teams, or other news service employees, for which the news outlets take editorial responsibility. Readers' comments or posts are commentaries written by laypersons, individuals who are consumers of news and typically are not employed by news outlets. Borrowing from the "internet language", in some cases, we refer to such individuals as users. In most cases, the media outlets do not take editorial responsibility for readers' comments, although they may require them to be compliant with the portal's rules and community standards.

6.1 Exploratory Analysis

We draw content from seven websites listed in Table 6.1. Three of them, Onet, WP, and Interia, are the most popular online news outlets in Poland. Gazeta.pl is a news portal closely linked to Gazeta Wyborcza, one of the largest Polish daily newspapers, whereas rp.pl is an electronic version of another major daily, Rzeczpospolita.[1] To this mix, we add two sources characterised by stronger ideological sentiments: the left-leaning natemat.pl and the right-leaning fronda.pl. As can be seen in Table 6.1, the seven outlets jointly attract nearly 48 million users per week which is a

[1] In June 2020, Gazeta Wyborcza had a daily circulation of around 86,000 paper copies and Rzeczpospolita of 53,000 paper copies.

Table 6.1 The seven internet sources

Website	*Real users per week (mln)*	*Daily page views per visitor*[a]	*Daily time on site*[a,b]	*First launched*	*Articles on FTAs*	*Comments*
fronda.pl	0.7[c]	1.8	02:57	Nov 2008	98	72
gazeta.pl	5.1[d]	2.04	03:18	Dec 1996	366	2742
interia.pl	6.3[d]	3.96	06:16	Nov 2000	369	93,446
onet.pl	13.5[d]	2.87	04:52	Jun 1996	743	n/a[e]
natemat.pl	2.5[f]	1.3	02:11	Feb 2012	91	493
rp.pl	4.9[d]	1.7	02:18	Mar 1997	651	1698
wp.pl	14.7[d]	2.96	04:57	Mar 1995	368	28,237
TOTAL	47.7				2686	126,688

[a] https://www.alexa.com/siteinfo/. [b] Average time that a visitor spends on site per day. [c] Badanie Gemius PBI, January 2019. [d] Badanie Gemius PBI, April 2020. [e] Onet.pl restricts users' ability to comment. [f] Natemat.pl reported having 10 million unique users over the whole month of January 2020, https://natemat.pl/298409, wyniki-ogladalnosci-natemat-pl-mamy juz-10-mln-unikalnych-uzytkownikow.

substantial number in a country with a population of 38.5 million.[2] Using the names of the seven trade agreements, we retrieve a total of 2686 unique articles published between 1995 and spring of 2019, which attracted 126,688 comments posted by readers.[3] To be included in our sample, the published online articles must count at least 300 words. A survey of the academic literature on the structure of newspaper and online articles published in recent years in the Polish language (e.g. Kasiak 2015 and 2016; Kula 2013 and 2014) showed that there is no standard or typical length for such texts and that there are no significant differences in the content, structure, and length between articles published in traditional newspapers and online outlets. Nevertheless, we decide to introduce the arbitrary threshold of minimum 300 words per article to increase the

[2] This is not the same as unique individuals as some users may visit more than one of those services within a week.

[3] Users can freely post comments to articles on six out of seven analysed portals. Onet is the only outlet that restricts the comment functionality. We searched each of the portal's online archives for articles mentioning any of the trade agreements' acronyms, that is CEFTA, CETA, GATT, NAFTA, TTIP, TPP, and WTO, which are commonly used in discussions in the Polish language. In our search, conducted in May 2019, we did not impose any time restrictions and thus obtained all relevant articles published online and dating back to the creation of each of the seven outlets. Each identified article was downloaded together with accompanying readers' comments.

likelihood that the analysed articles contain a minimum of key facts and information as well as their interpretation or opinions on the matter of FTAs. We do not introduce any length limits on the comments made by readers.

Although our sample covers the period from 1995 onwards, there are only four articles published before 2000, all of them in gazeta.pl—focusing on CEFTA (three articles) and GATT (one article), whereas the latest article was published on 13 May 2019. The early articles were published when the Polish internet was in its infancy, with relatively few people being able to access online content, and commenting functionality was not widely available. Consequently, the first reader's comment in our database comes from 1 September 2003. The chosen period means that our sample is temporarily skewed towards the 2010s: it includes only 195 articles published between 1995 and 2008, compared to 2491 articles published between 2009 and May 2019. However, we have decided to keep the observations from the earlier years as this allows us to investigate the dynamics of the debate and changes in the attitudes towards free trade throughout the Polish economic transformation from a rather closed and centrally planned economy to an open market economy, as well as observe how the role of online media in the economic discourse has evolved since their inception in the 1990s.

Going back to Table 6.1, we can see that while Onet published the largest number of FTA-related articles, it was Interia that attracted the vast majority of readers' comments (74% of all comments). Not surprisingly, the latter also appears to have the most "attentive" visitors who, on average, visit four pages and spend six minutes on Interia.pl a day—those figures are significantly larger than for any other service. The two "ideological" outlets, fronda.pl and natemat.pl, published the fewest articles and consequently had the fewest comments. Although this is most likely due to their much later launch dates and smaller size compared to the other portals with larger editorial teams and readerships.

The most frequently written about FTA was TTIP, which attracted nearly half of all online comments, followed by CETA (see Table 6.2). On average, an article attracted 47 user comments. The ratio of comments per article is the highest for CETA—nearly 121 comments per article on average, distancing TTIP which attracted on average 51 comments per article. The least comment-heavy were CEFTA and WTO, perhaps because they were "done deals" during the analysed period. The distribution of articles

Table 6.2 Articles and comments by FTA

	CEFTA	*CETA*	*GATT*	*NAFTA*	*TTIP*	*TPP*	*WTO*
Articles	30	357	46	168	1173	119	793
Comments	116	43,083	926	4049	59,899	3714	14,901
Comments per article	3.9	120.7	20.1	24.1	51.1	31.2	18.8

and comments concerning each of the FTAs is discussed in more detail in section 6.3.

The number of online publications depends on two dynamic factors. The first one is the demand for such content. With the low internet penetration in Poland in the 1990s and 2000s[4], there was a relatively small market for online news. Consequently, as mentioned above, relatively few FTA-related articles were published online in those years. The supply of online content discussing the seven FTAs shoots up in the second decade of the twenty-first century, when Fig. 6.1 shows an increase in the quarterly number of trade-related publications which is likely to be driven by an increasing online readership, new players joining our sample of outlets, and the second key factor, the increased public interest driven by negotiations of several high profile and controversial FTAs. We observe that the number of publications begins to grow rapidly from the point when the TTIP negotiations begin in 2013 and reaches its peak in 2016 when there was a culmination of headline-grabbing events related to CETA and TTIP.

6.2 Media and Internet Popularity of FTAs in Poland and Other Countries

One of the questions to consider is whether the dynamics of the media and public interest in the FTAs are unique to Poland or perhaps they could be generalised to other countries. To shed some light on this issue, in Fig. 6.1 we compare the quarterly counts of articles in the seven Polish internet outlets with the corresponding numbers published in English, German, and French newspapers. The data on the latter is taken from ProQuest

[4] The first dial-up service enabling household access to the internet was introduced in April 1996. From that point the internet penetration started increasing gradually, and internet reached approximately a third of households in 2005, 63.4% in 2010, and 84.2% in 2018 (Statistics Poland, 2019).

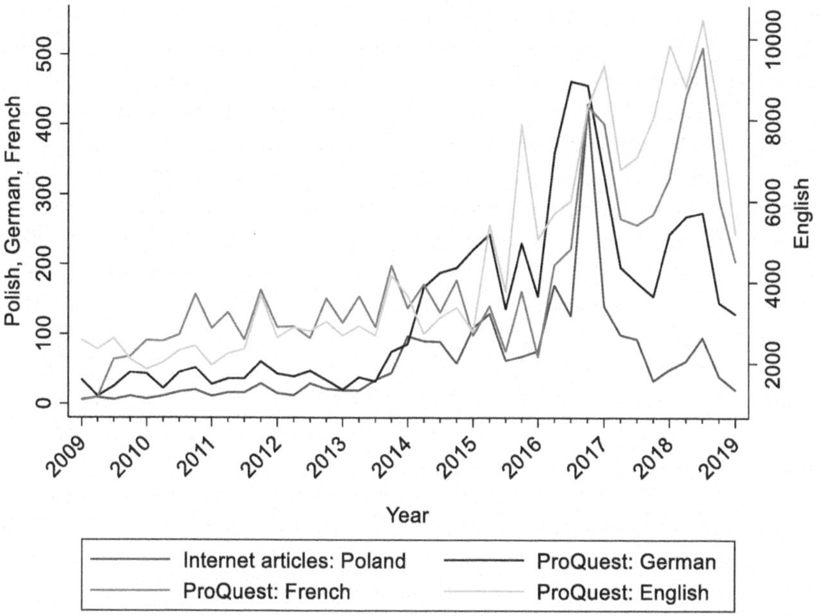

Fig. 6.1 Frequency of articles mentioning the analysed FTAs

Newspapers which lists 2024 English, 11 German, and 40 French titles.[5] Comparing the Polish online outlets with traditional newspapers might not be ideal and, thus, should be taken with caution, but it offers a simple and intuitive way to demonstrate that the Polish media's interest in the FTAs appears to follow patterns similar to those in other countries. It has to be strongly emphasised that comparing the absolute numbers of articles presented in Fig. 6.1 does not make much sense as they are based on very different numbers of newspapers outlets. For example, it is reasonable to expect 40 French newspapers to produce more such articles than 11 German newspapers or seven Polish internet outlets. Instead, we should

[5] We take 2009 as a starting point as this is the first year for which ProQuest Newspapers offers a broad coverage of the German and French titles—prior to that year only a small number of titles is listed. Unfortunately, ProQuest Newspapers lists only one Polish daily, Gazeta Wyborcza, which means that using it to represent the popularity of the FTA topics in the Polish media would be grossly unreliable, and this is why we resort to using our online sample for the comparison purposes in Fig. 6.1. Similarly, ProQuest's coverage of Italian newspapers is not sufficient to include Italy in our comparison.

focus on the shapes of the curves representing quarterly numbers of FTA articles in the four languages. They tend to rise and drop within the same quarters—this is very clearly visible, for example, in the fourth quarter of 2011, the second quarter of 2015, or the third quarter of 2016. The correlation coefficients between the series representing the Polish articles and those in the other three languages range from 0.5 for English to 0.81 for German. These high values support the assertion that the media's interest in the FTAs in the four countries follows similar trends and dynamics, and that news outlets across those countries find the FTAs noteworthy at the same time. Consequently, it is possible that the patterns observed in Poland could be generalised to other countries.

Next, we are going to compare internet users' interest in the FTAs. Figure 6.2 displays the cumulative Google Trends scores for online searches of acronyms associated with each of the seven FTAs, globally and for four European countries, including Poland.[6] In essence, the service analyses the popularity of Google search queries across countries, regions, and languages, which leads us to treat those scores as a proxy measure of the demand for information about the seven FTAs. Google Trends captures the internet users' interest in particular topics within specified periods and displays it as a normalised score ranging from 0 to 100.[7] In Fig. 6.2, we present values that are a sum of individual Google Trends scores associated with each of the seven FTAs within each month between January 2004 and June 2020. A cursory glimpse on Fig. 6.2 reveals that the popularity and patterns of the internet searches are fairly similar across the geographic locations. Despite differing domestic agendas within each of the countries, internet users appear to demonstrate a fairly similar demand for information about the FTAs. The scores for Poland are hardly discernible from the global, German, and French ones. This is confirmed by high correlation coefficients, which for Poland range from 0.62 with

[6] For Germany, Italy, Poland, and worldwide the joint score is a sum of individual, country-level, Google Trends scores associated with searches for the acronyms CEFTA, CETA, GATT, NAFTA, TPP, TTIP, and WTO, which are most commonly used in those languages to refer to those agreements. For France we replaced WTO with OMC, NAFTA with ALENA, and CEFTA with ALECE, which appear to be predominantly used in the French language.

[7] More information about Google Trends can be found at https://support.google.com/trends/answer/4365533?hl=en. The service itself can be accessed at https://trends.google.com/.

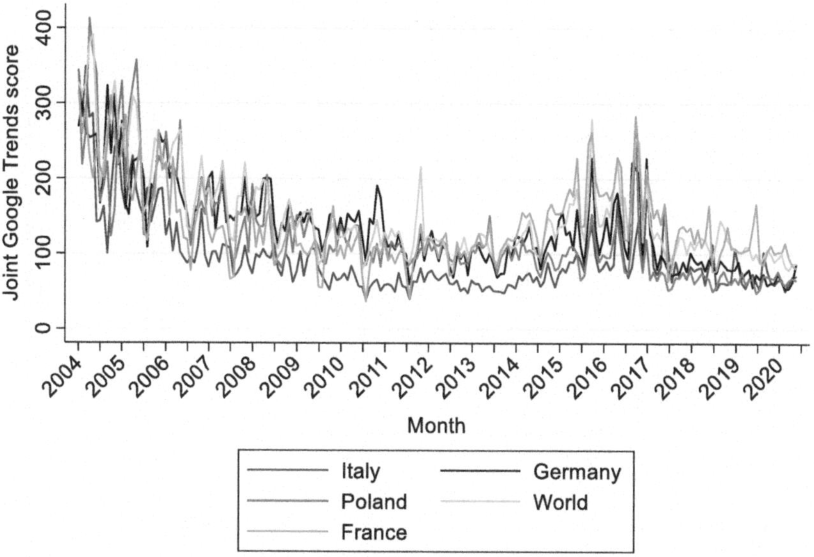

Fig. 6.2 Popularity of trade agreements in internet searches

France, through 0.8 with Germany to 0.86 with the global Google Trends scores.

This basic analysis suggests that the intensity, dynamics, and demand for the discussion about the seven FTAs analysed in this book follow similar patterns, or peaks and troughs, in Poland and the other countries, both in terms of location and in terms of language. This is not surprising because although different countries may have different domestic agendas and local news focus, their media outlets and inhabitants do not exist in a vacuum—they also follow the international economic and political agendas as well as pay attention to global trends and developments. This should be particularly true for issues related to international trade and FTAs as they simultaneously affect economies and citizens of multiple countries. Even though this chapter focuses solely on the Polish online debate, its similarity to the debates showed elsewhere in this section suggests that our key findings could possibly be generalised to other countries. Nevertheless, any such generalisations should be made cautiously and take into consideration any local and domestic conditions and intricacies.

6.3 The FTA Narrative

As Fig. 6.3 shows, each of the discussed agreements attracted media interest over time and was surrounded by its own narrative. The sentiment of those narratives is discussed later in this chapter. For now, we focus on the

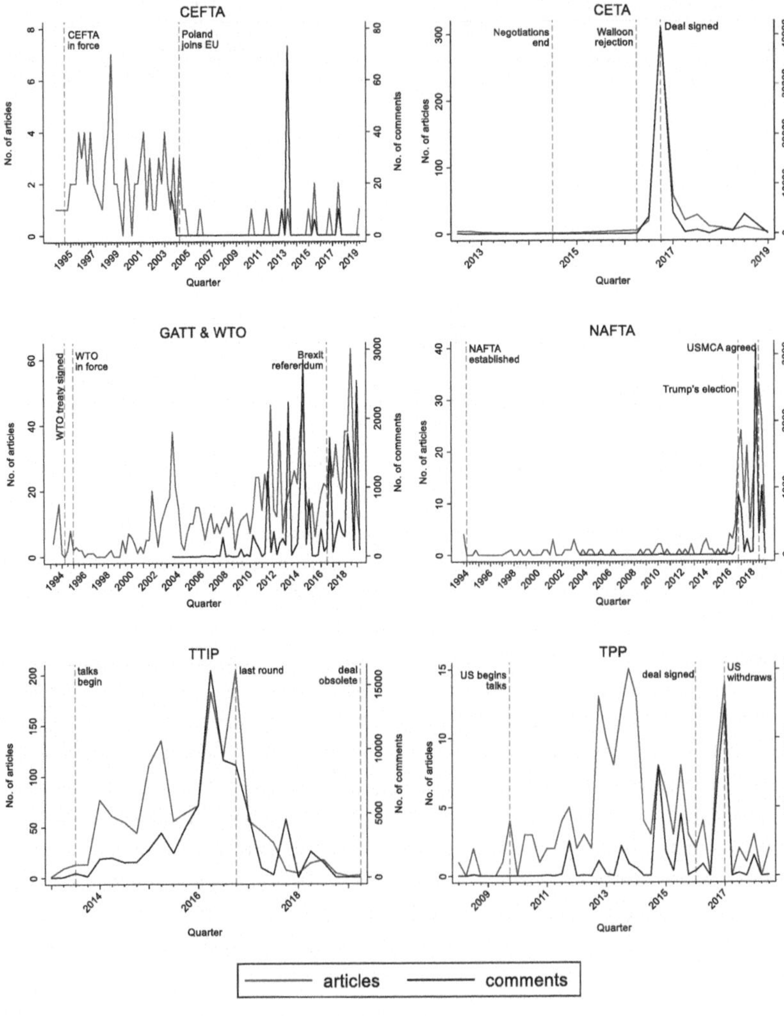

Fig. 6.3 Articles and comments by FTA. *Source: Own elaboration*

amount of attention each FTA received, measured by the numbers of online articles and readers' comments published in each quarter. The first observation is that, indeed, the spikes in journalists' and readers' interest appear to coincide with key events, such as negotiations, ratifications, protests, associated with each of the agreements (see Fig. 2.8 in Chap. 2 for the timeline of events). For example, CEFTA attracted the greatest amount of attention during the period of Poland's membership. There is also a pronounced spike in the number of articles between 1997 and 1999 when Romania and Bulgaria joined the bloc, providing newsworthy material. Following Poland's membership of the EU, and thus the departure from CEFTA, there was relatively little interest in the agreement. The sudden spike in users' comments in 2013 coincides with Croatia's departure from CEFTA when the country joined the EU. CEFTA did not grasp as much online attention as the other agreements, but this does not mean that the agreement was not important to the Poles, simply the period of its greatest relevance to Poland was when the country's internet was in its infancy. Similarly, CETA received the greatest attention around the time when the drama of the Walloon rejection was unfolding, and the culmination was reached when the problem was resolved, and CETA signed in late 2016. In comparison, NAFTA reached the heights of 20–40 articles per quarter following President Donald Trump's election, his resounding criticism of the deal and the declarations of American withdrawal from the bloc. This reinvigorated interest in NAFTA was topped by the intensity of coverage that the ratification of the US–Mexico–Canada Agreement, USMCA, received in 2018.

Robert Shiller (2019), a Nobel Prize-winning economist, refers to the science of epidemiology to explain the spread of interest in economic narratives. He argues that economic narratives (to which news of FTAs belong) follow the same pattern as a spread of disease. As an FTA or some related issue surfaces, we observe first mentions in the news, which are then followed by a "contagion" stage during which the public's interest in learning more about the topic increases and journalists create more content to reach as many readers as possible[8]. Over time, the number of informed (*infected* by the narrative) individuals rises, but they gradually begin to lose interest (become *immune*). As the issue stops being a novel

[8] Whether the production of news articles is driven by public interest or the public interest drives content creation is an interesting question which we will not attempt to answer in this book.

topic in social interactions, demand for reading more news, or commenting, about the FTA begins to diminish. The "epidemic" also weakens because the number of individuals that have still not been exposed to the news is declining and an increasing share of the non-informed individuals is not susceptible to the "infection", or simply not interested in learning about free trade. Thus, journalists' attention moves to a new topic that the public finds novel and appealing.

This epidemic-like transmission mechanism can often be depicted by a hump-shaped curve apparent in five out of six diagrams in Fig. 6.3. Only the GATT and WTO diagram does not appear to follow this pattern. The interest in GATT and WTO appears to wane and increase, and then wane and increase again. This is probably driven by the fact that together they constitute the founding block for the other trade agreements. Thus, they are frequently invoked when other trade deals, or the lack thereof, are discussed (this can also be seen in Table 6.3). In addition, the WTO's dispute settlement system and arbitration are often referred to in the news on trade disagreements between countries. Following the Brexit referendum of 2016, WTO received much attention in the context of "falling back on the WTO rules" which surfaced as an alternative to reaching a trade deal with the European Union (Morris 2019). In the case of CEFTA, the epidemic-like contagion pattern is not that clear, although it cannot be ruled out, as the agreement reached peaks of its interest and relevance to the Poles in the 1990s when news outlets had limited online presence.

None of the analysed FTAs happened in a vacuum or was talked about without references to other deals, elements of international trade, economy, politics, or society in general. In other words, discussions on our FTAs were happening in particular contexts and often shared some common themes. Following Shiller's (2019) example, we could say that debates around each of the FTAs form a part of a larger constellation of narratives. For example, the newsworthiness of NAFTA in Poland was boosted by the narrative of President Donald Trump and his policies. The public interest in the newly elected US president's words and actions led to an increased interest in some of his policies, including the criticism and renegotiation of NAFTA. Undoubtedly, an important part of a narrative constellation surrounding an FTA will be the narratives associated with other, earlier or concurring, FTAs. Table 6.3 shows the co-occurrence of the FTA names in the analysed samples of online articles, readers' comments, and research publications discussed in Chap. 5. In other words, it shows what percentage of articles or comments listed in the left-hand side

Table 6.3 Co-occurrence of FTA terms in online articles, comments, and academic research outputs

Mentioned FTA	*Co-occurring FTA (also mentioned)*						
	GATT	*WTO*	*NAFTA*	*CEFTA*	*CETA*	*TTIP*	*TPP*
a. Online articles							
GATT		74%	15%	0%	8%	9%	0%
WTO	4%		6%	0%	2%	11%	0%
NAFTA	2%	17%		0%	17%	38%	5%
CEFTA	0%	0%	0%		0%	0%	0%
CETA	1%	4%	10%	0%		49%	1%
TTIP	0%	8%	10%	0%	22%		3%
TPP	0%	2%	11%	0%	3%	26%	
b. Readers' comments							
GATT		29%	0%	0%	57%	71%	14%
WTO	1%		1%	0%	0%	2%	1%
NAFTA	0%	1%		1%	29%	20%	1%
CEFTA	0%	0%	0%		30%	26%	0%
CETA	0%	0%	1%	0%		18%	0%
TTIP	0%	0%	1%	0%	36%		1%
TPP	1%	2%	1%	0%	17%	16%	
c. Academic articles[a]							
GATT		100%	26%	0%	5%	32%	21%
WTO	59%		16%	0%	6%	31%	19%
NAFTA	45%	45%		0%	18%	36%	27%
CEFTA	0%	0%	0%		0%	0%	0%
CETA	17%	33%	33%	0%		50%	17%
TTIP	38%	63%	25%	0%	19%		19%
TPP	67%	100%	50%	0%	17%	50%	

The percentage points indicate what share of all outputs mentioning an FTA indicated in the first column also mention one of the other FTAs indicated in the remaining columns.

[a] Based on the sample of 51 research outputs discussed in Chap. 5.

column labelled "Mentioned FTA" contain references to any of the other six FTAs indicated in the remaining columns. For example, we can see that 74% of all online articles mentioning GATT also mention WTO. However, only 4% of the articles that mention WTO also mention GATT.

A quick look at Table 6.3 reveals that academic authors (panel c) are significantly more likely to refer to multiple FTAs in their work. All articles in our sample that mention GATT or TPP also mention WTO. Notably, WTO and GATT tend to appear in a relatively large share of articles discussing the other FTAs. This is not surprising because both agreements are often referred to as benchmarks or templates for latter trade agreements. Other pairs of deals that closely "coexist" in the academic literature include CETA and TTIP, TPP and TTIP, and NAFTA and TTIP. Overall, the average "co-occurrence value", a simple average of the percentage values shown in the table, for academic articles is 26%, which is three times higher than for online articles as well as readers' comments.

In contrast, WTO and, especially, GATT are not so readily recalled by journalists and readers in their texts—very few articles and comments focused on other FTAs refer to either of the two "benchmark" agreements. It is clear that in popular media four agreements, NAFTA, CETA, TTIP, and TPP, form a narrative constellation of their own as both online articles or comments mentioning any of these deals are likely to include references to the other three. The basis of this constellation is likely to be the temporal proximity of the trade negotiations (or re-negotiations in the NAFTA's case) of those agreements as well as the overlapping geographic coverage. Canada and the United States are involved in three whereas the European Union and therefore Poland are in two of those deals. In particular, the narratives of CETA and TTIP, both affecting Poland, appear to feed off each other in the Polish public debate in 2016–2017 when they attracted multiple headline-grabbing events (see also Gawronska-Nowak et al. 2019). The existence of the constellation of four FTAs is further demonstrated by the sudden spike in readers' commenting activity in Fig. 6.4. The four "hot" years for those four deals, 2015–2018, saw 109,508 comments posted which accounts for 86% of all comments in our sample. This suggests that frequent news of free trade negotiations may have led to increased readers' engagement with such news, enticing or persuading them to form their own opinions and share them publicly with others.

Interestingly, CEFTA appears to be an outlier in Table 6.3. Neither news nor academic articles mentioning CEFTA refer to any other agreement. Some cross-referencing appears only in the online comments—readers seem to link it to CETA and TTIP. However, one must be very careful making this link as all those co-occurrences appeared in a handful of comments published in 2015 and 2016, so they might be an effect of spelling errors or unawareness of the distinction between CEFTA and CETA among the readers. Thus, it appears that the CEFTA's narrative functions in relative isolation and does not form a part of the constellations encompassing the other FTAs.

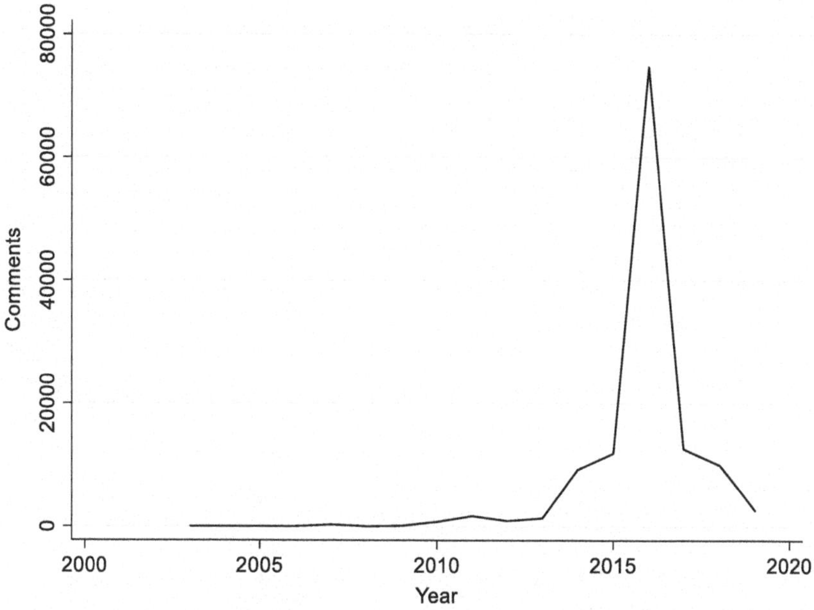

Fig. 6.4 Readers' comments by year

Narratives, including those surrounding free trade, form constellations because they appeal to similar recipients' interests, needs, or experiences, but also because their credibility and attractiveness may rely on a set of other, linked, narratives. They may free the recipient from the effort of updating her knowledge or verifying facts, as taking one plausible narrative for granted may provide a reasonable basis for accepting another, similar, narrative. This practice may eventually lead to the creation of conventional wisdom, which guides so many of people's daily activities. The lesson here is that our FTAs are likely to be a part of broader constellations of free trade and economic narratives, and we need to be mindful of that broader picture if we want to understand the content and sentiment contained in the FTA debates.

6.4 Expert Knowledge in the Online Content

The articles and comments are representations of narratives surrounding certain events, facts or, in our case, trade agreements. Shiller (2019) notes that such narratives can significantly impact individuals' behaviour and, therefore, translate into real economic outcomes, both at micro and at macro levels. In the remainder of this chapter, we investigate the extent to which those narratives are rooted in expert knowledge and how they are driven by sentiments and emotions.

We begin by scrutinising the expert knowledge indicators in the sample of articles and their accompanying readers' comments. This part relies on the Expert Knowledge Dictionary (EKD) constructed in Chap. 5 and natural language processing tools for Polish. As a brief reminder, EKD is based on a sample of 51 academic research outputs published in Polish between 1994 and 2019 and consists of specialist vocabulary related to economics, free trade, and FTAs that are commonly encountered in the academic literature but seldom used outside of the expert debate as well as some "common knowledge" terms which are frequently used both inside and outside of academic discussions surrounding FTAs, for example food standards, GMO, trade, intellectual property. To perform the analysis, we utilise the Natural Language Toolkit (NLTK) for Python[9] in conjunction with the morphological analyser for the Polish language—Morfeusz 2 (Kieraś and Woliński 2017; Woliński 2014)[10].

Our analytical procedure takes an article or a comment as a unit of observation and follows five steps. First, the text of each article or comment is read in, cleaned of redundant elements, and the number of words counted. We also keep track of publication dates, outlets, and primary FTA discussed. Second, within the text, we search for EKD terms in any of the inflected forms found in the academic literature in Chap. 5. Third, we use the Morfeusz 2 module and perform a morphological analysis to determine lexemes, or basic lexical units, of all words in the text. In step four, we take the lemmatised text, in which all words have been replaced by corresponding lexemes, and look for terms from the lemmatised

[9] NLTK is a freely available comprehensive platform for processing human language data. More information can be found at https://www.nltk.org/.

[10] Morfeusz 2 is a software module designed for morphological analysis of text in Polish with tools for a range of programming languages, including Python. In our analysis we use Morfeusz version 22.11.2020. More information and examples can be found at http://morfeusz.sgjp.pl/.

version of EKD. The third and fourth steps are crucial for any meaningful analysis due to the high complexity of the Polish syntax and grammar—a challenge previously encountered by Bień and Szafran (2001), and Rybak et al. (2020), among others. Considering the lemmatised versions allows us to catch all, or at least the vast majority, of inflected forms of all terms incorporated in EKD. Finally, we collate and export the extracted information which contains both counts and instances of indicators of expert knowledge organised by units of observation, that is online articles or readers' comments.

Tables 6.4 and 6.5 summarise the basic indicators of expert knowledge in the online articles and readers' comments, respectively. Additionally, Table 6.4 compares these results to the expert literature. The indicators are calculated for the whole analysed period as well as two sub-periods: before and after the Great Recession of 2008. It ought to be noted that the small size of the pre-2008 sub-samples relative to the post-2008 period

Table 6.4 Basic indicators of expert knowledge: comparison between the expert literature and online articles

	Expert literature[a]				*Online articles (popular media)*			
	Mean	*SD*	*Min*	*Max*	*Mean*	*SD*	*Min*	*Max*
Period (sample size)	1994–2019 (*N* = 51)				1995–2019 (*N* = 2686)			
Number of all words	4800	1948	1298	10,101	841	625	300	7221
Words belonging to EKD	539	246	146	1177	45	36.6	0	336
Percentage of EKD words	11.4%	3.1%	6%	19.4%	5.9%	3.4%	0%	18.5%
Unique EKD terms	142	47	66	254	27	17.5	0	124
Period (sample size)	1994–2008 (*N* = 14)				1995–2008 (*N* = 195)			
Number of all words	4622	1619	2428	7875	1036	912	301	4576
Words belonging to EKD	503	245	146.0	1177	66	58	1	312
Percentage of EKD words	10.9%	3.2%	6%	15.6%	7.1%	4.1%	0.2%	18.1%
Unique EKD terms	134	55	66	254	34	23	1	106
Period (sample size)	2009–2019 (*N* = 37)				2009–2019 (*N* = 2,491)			
Number of all words	4868	2075	1298	10,101	825	595	300	7221
Words belonging to EKD	552	249	173	1114	44	34	0	336
Percentage of EKD words	11.5%	3%	6.7%	19.4%	5.8%	3.3%	0%	18.5%
Unique EKD terms	145	44	71	254	26	17	0	124

[a] The sample of 51 research outputs discussed in Chap. 5.

SD = standard deviation.

Table 6.5 Basic indicators of expert knowledge in readers' comments

	All comments				*Comments containing EKD terms*			
	Mean	*SD*	*Min*	*Max*	*Mean*	*SD*	*Min*	*Max*
Period (sample size)	2003–2019 (*N* = 126,688)				2003–2019 (*N* = 27,348)			
Number of all words	23	29	1	1318	44	46	1	1318
Words belonging to EKD	0.46	1.44	0	83	2.15	2.45	1	83
Percentage of EKD words	1.5%	3.9%	0%	100%	6.8%	5.9%	0.2%	100%
Unique EKD terms	0.41	1.15	0	43	1.88	1.82	1	43
Period (sample size)	2003–2008 (*N* = 364)				2003–2008 (*N* = 80)			
Number of all words	24	23	1	109	44	26	6	109
Words belonging to EKD	0.38	0.9	0	6	1.74	1.14	1	6
Percentage of EKD words	1.3%	3.4%	0%	28.6%	5.8%	5.3%	0.9%	28.6%
Unique EKD terms	0.35	0.80	0	5	1.59	0.96	1	5
Period (sample size)	2009–2019 (*N* = 126,324)				2009–2019 (*N* = 27,268)			
Number of all words	23	29	1	1318	44	46	1	1318
Words belonging to EKD	0.46	1.44	0	83	2.15	2.45	1	83
Percentage of EKD words	1.5%	3.9%	0%	100%	6.8%	5.9%	0.2%	100%
Unique EKD terms	0.41	1.15	0	43	1.88	1.82	1	43

SD = standard deviation.

means that the overall indicators (1994/5–2019) are driven largely by materials published during the latter sub-period.

The comparison of the expert literature and online news articles yields expected results. Academic outputs are on average five times longer than those written by journalists and exhibit significantly higher content of expert vocabulary. When we look at the percentage of EKD words in all words, a typical academic article contains nearly twice as many expert words as the share found in an average online article (11.4% vs. 5.9%). Moreover, some of the articles in popular media seem not to contain any EKD terms that would signal linkages to expert knowledge. Researchers also demonstrate a much broader range of expert vocabulary used—their texts contain on average five times more unique expert terms than popular articles (142 vs. 27). The expert knowledge content also appears to be more consistent across the academic works. The standard deviation indicators, which measure how dispersed or spread out individual observations are from the sample averages, are smaller than the mean for academic articles in all rows of Table 6.4. For example, the average distance between the values of the percentage of EKD words of individual outputs and the corresponding means are over 3% for both academic and news articles. However, those standard deviations represent only a quarter of the average share of the EKD words in academic articles (3.1% ÷ 11.4% = 0.27), compared to well over a half for news articles (3.4% ÷ 5.9% = 0.58). Thus, while the measures of expert vocabulary in expert literature tend to be fairly close to the mean, suggesting some consistent content of expert knowledge across the academic articles on average, they are significantly more spread out and on average further away from the mean within the popular media sample. This means that the sample is more varied and consists of relatively large numbers of news articles with comparatively low expert content and articles with high expert content. We can reach a similar conclusion when we consider the appearance of unique EKD terms in both types of texts—popular media articles appear to be more of a "mixed bag" than their academic counterparts also in that respect.

When we compare the outputs published until 2008 to those published from 2009 onward, we do not observe statistically significant differences between the indicators for the academic articles. Their average length and content of the EKD terms increased, but the changes are rather marginal. In contrast, articles in the popular media got shorter by approximately a fifth as the average length dropped from 1036 to 825 words. We also note a reduction of a similar magnitude in the expert knowledge content in the latter period. The average share of EKD terms in the news articles dropped from 7.1% to 5.8%, and the average number of unique EKD terms appearing in an article fell from 34 to 26. Thus, while the academic authors remained consistent in their use of expert vocabulary, we observe a significantly reduced reliance on expert terminology and presumably expert knowledge in the news articles. There are several potential explanations for this change. It could be the case that journalists began using a simpler language in recent years and reduced their use of expert jargon to make their texts more appealing to the general public without reducing the conveyed amount and quality of expert knowledge. However, our in-depth review of a sample of articles spanning the two sub-periods does not confirm this (see Chap. 7). It is also possible that the changes in the news media market forced by the increasing role of online services, which have led to fiercer competition and a decline of traditional newspapers, have exacerbated pressures on news teams—forcing them to produce instant, more frequent, and more reader-engaging content. This is likely to have reduced the time and space available to journalists for consulting expert sources and performing in-depth analyses of discussed problems

Interviews with researchers specialising in economics, international trade, international relations, or related disciplines, and references to their research work and opinions constitute another likely avenue of relaying expert knowledge. Consequently, mentions of researchers' names in online articles could serve as another indicator of expert knowledge. We scan our corpus of popular media for occurrences of names of 156 Polish academics whose works on FTAs are listed on Google Scholar—we go beyond the sample on which EKD is based (see Chap. 5) and consider all authors who produced FTA-related outputs between 1994 and 2019. It turns out that only 37, or around 1.4% of all analysed articles, contain any references to academic researchers. This share remains similarly low across the 1995–2008 and 2009–2019 sub-samples. Thus, researchers and their work do not appear to be a direct source of knowledge for journalists writing about free trade.

Table 6.5 reports the results of an analogous exercise for the readers' comments to the online articles. We note that the first such comments appeared in 2003 and the commenting activity was low in the early years. We observe an average of only 61 comments per year until 2008, the average increases drastically to over 12,000 comments per year for years 2009–2019. Thus, our results and discussion are unquestionably driven by readers' activity during the second sub-period. Another striking observation is that the vast majority of comments does not contain any EKD terms. Therefore, in Table 6.5, we separate results for the comments that contain at least a single EKD term (21.6% of the total) from all comments. The posts containing indicators of expert knowledge appear to be twice as long as those without EKD terms.[11] Thus, readers who express educated opinions and arguments appear to put more effort and words into composing their posts.

Interestingly, in this category, the content of expert knowledge relative to the text length is higher than in the online articles: on average 6.8% of all words in readers' "educated" comments belong to EKD, compared to 5.9% in the news articles (Table 6.4). Nevertheless, the relationship between the post or article length and its content of EKD terms is not that clear and likely to hold only to a certain point. As shown in Fig. 6.5, the

[11] The high standard deviations associated with the length of readers' comments tell us that the numbers of words in individual posts vary greatly from the mean, that is we observe a large number of very short posts consisting of just a few words and then there is a considerable group of longer and more elaborate comments.

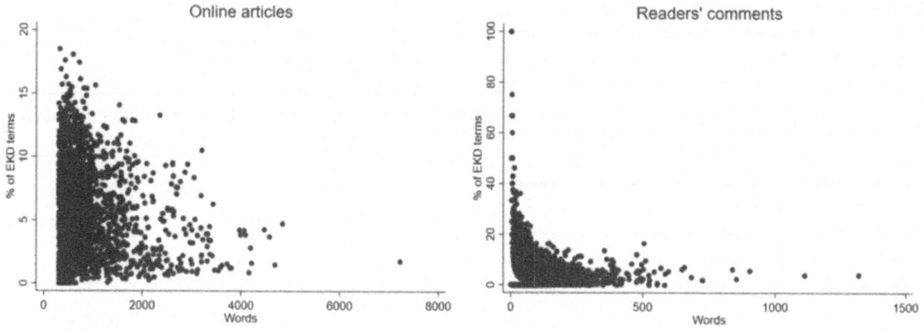

Fig. 6.5 Share of EKD terms and text length. *Source: Own elaboration*

percentage share of EKD terms in text decreases in text length, both for articles and comments. Although longer texts tend to contain relatively fewer expert terms, they do not necessarily convey a smaller amount of expert knowledge. Their greater length could be a product of authors' more elaborate writing style, a provision of some additional background, not necessarily expert, information or an intention to use simpler language to explain key terminology, facts, and arguments in laypersons' terms.

Overall, we can say that there is a core of highly informed readers whose comments are substantive and arguments rooted in expert knowledge, and this does not appear to have changed across the two sub-periods even though the length of journalists' articles and their expert content declined over time.

6.4.1 *Heterogeneity of Results Across FTAs and Media Outlets*

In Tables 6.6 and 6.7, we inspect whether the content of expert knowledge in online articles and readers' comments is comparable across individual FTAs and media outlets, respectively. Our aim is to identify potential outliers in our analysis. We observe that articles about the "old" deals, namely, GATT, NAFTA, and CEFTA, were significantly longer than those focusing on the other FTAs. A large share of those articles was written in the pre-2008 period when online news articles were on average longer than those written after 2008 when deals such as CETA, TTIP, and TPP hit the headlines (see Table 6.4). When we look at the percentage of EKD words appearing in text, we note that it ranges from 5.73% to 7.95% for articles and 1.05% to 2.09% for readers' comments for most deals. The

Table 6.6 Expert knowledge content by FTA

FTA	*Online articles*		*Readers' comments (all)*	
	Average length (words)	*Percentage of EKD words*	*Average length (words)*	*Percentage of EKD words*
GATT	1072	7.95%	29.4	2.09%
WTO	807	6.52%	24.8	1.54%
NAFTA	1040	5.73%	19.7	1.36%
CEFTA	1553	6.24%	25.8	1.05%
CETA	804	6.13%	20.9	1.48%
TTIP	881	6.43%	23.9	1.48%
TPP	759	2.71%	24.4	0.77%

Table 6.7 Expert content knowledge by media outlets

Online media outlet	*Online articles*		*Readers' comments (all)*	
	Average length (words)	*Percentage of EKD words*	*Average length (words)*	*Percentage of EKD words*
fronda.pl	1149	4.03%	52.5	1.9%
gazeta.pl	1156	6.24%	38.4	2.42%
interia.pl	734	7.57%	20.6	1.58%
natemat.pl	819	5.20%	35.3	1.17%
onet.pl	816	5.75%	n/a	
rp.pl	745	6.08%	63.8	2.3%
wp.pl	777	4.58%	26.2	0.94%

discussions of GATT and WTO appear to be the best rooted in expert knowledge—perhaps because they received a relatively consistent amount of attention over the years (see Fig. 6.3) and have constituted a benchmark for comparing other deals, meaning that individuals writing about free trade and appraising other FTAs have stronger incentives to obtain a more in-depth knowledge of GATT and WTO.

TPP is a clear outlier, both articles and comments on TPP are characterised by a notably lower share of expert terminology. This could be due to the fact that TPP is geographically distant—it does not affect Poland directly so the local knowledge about the deal is likely to be limited as individuals may see little benefit in spending their time and energy on learning about the deal's details. NAFTA is the only other FTA that does not involve Poland and is also characterised by a below-average expert knowledge content. However, its indicators of expert knowledge are not nearly as low as in the case of TPP. There are two explanations for this. First, some of the NAFTA texts were written before 2009, in the first subperiod, when journalists were more likely to rely on expert terminology (see Table 6.4). Second, unlike TPP, NAFTA is often discussed in conjunction with TTIP, WTO, and CETA (see Table 6.3) which attract above-average levels of expert vocabulary.

Table 6.7 presents analogous information organised by popular media outlets. The best-performing in terms of expert knowledge appear to be the two popular mainstream outlets: interia.pl and gazeta.pl. The latter also exhibits the highest content of the EKD words in its readers' comments. In contrast, another mainstream portal, wp.pl, performs poorly with the second-lowest expert terminology content in articles and the lowest in readers' posts. However, it is the performance of the two "ideological" outlets that is most interesting. The right-leaning fronda.pl shows the lowest content of expert knowledge in their texts, although the content of expert terms in their readers' comments is above the average, whereas the left-leaning natemat.pl has expert knowledge content below average in both articles and readers' comments. This is consistent with our expectations that the content published in outlets with a stronger ideological hue would express stronger, more polarising opinions which are driven by emotions rather than objective expert knowledge. We investigate this further in Chap. 7.

6.4.2 *Types and Categories of Most Frequently Debated Issues*

Out of 1540 unique EKD terms identified in Chap. 5, we encounter 631 in online articles and 473 in readers' comments. As expected, the expert vocabulary used by both journalists and readers is relatively limited compared to that used in international trade research. We divide the EKD terms into eight broad categories. Although this process is somewhat subjective because some terms could be included in more than one category and, in some cases, the categorisation depends on context, it offers a reasonable attempt to capture issues which are of importance to researchers (experts), journalists, and typical readers. The eight categories are:

1. Agriculture—terms linked to agriculture, farming, and food production, for example *food safety*, *farming product*, *farming subsidy*, *GMO*, *Phytosanitary*.

2. Consumers and workers—terms relating to consumer, worker, and individual welfare, for example *workplace*, *employee rights*, *workforce*, *professional training*, *employment*, *trade union*, *consumer protection*, but also *human rights*, *poverty*, and *welfare*.
3. Environment and health protection—for example *health care*, *environmental protection*, *pollution*.
4. Legal, negotiations, and international relations—terms relating to legal aspects of agreements, their negotiations or international relations in general (including international organisations), for example *legal document*, *international relations actor*, *arbiter*, *World Bank*, *bilateral relations*, *clause*, *organisation member*, *de minimis*, *Doha round*, *single undertaking*, *negotiating strategy*, and *signatory*.
5. Macroeconomy—terms relating to the general performance and conditions of national and international economies, for example *economic growth*, *growth rate*, *economic transition*, *unemployment*, *the balance of trade*, *public budget*, *global crisis*, *inflation*, *economic cycle*.
6. Research and analysis—terms indicating undertaken research or a similar analytical process, for example *analysis*, *study*, *research evidence*, *economics*, *empirical*, *institute*, *Nobel Laureate*, *evaluations*, and *statistical*.
7. Trade and business—terms related directly to international trade exchanges and business activities, for example *trade barriers*, *tariff-free*, *industry*, *tariff*, *price*, *production inputs*, *profit*, *supplier*, *market access*, *free trade*, *competition*, and *quota*.
8. Other—terms which do not fall under or cross any of the above categories.

Table 6.8 displays the relative sizes of the term categories within each body of material (percentage share of the number of unique terms belonging to a category divided by the total number of all unique terms found in a given body of material) and the frequency with which terms appear in the texts. We distinguish two sub-periods for the expert literature and online articles: before and after the Great Recession of 2008. We omit this distinction for the readers' comments as there were few of those before 2009. For example, out of all unique, that is irrespective of whether they appear only once or more times, expert terms found in the body of academic literature, 4.59% belong to the agriculture category. When we consider multiple occurrences of the same terms, then agriculture accounts for 3.42% of all EKD terms used in research works between 1994 and 2008.

Table 6.8 Term categories: relative category size and frequency of term occurrence

Category	*Expert literature*[a]				*Online articles (popular media)*				*Readers' comments*	
	Terms (%)	*Occurrences (%)*			*Terms (%)*	*Occurrences (%)*			*Terms (%)*	*Occurr. (%)*
		1994–2008	*2009–2019*	*1994–2019*		*1995–2008*	*2009–2019*	*1995–2019*		
Agriculture	4.59	3.42	5.89	5.25	5.39	6.88	3.50	3.89	6.93	9.66
Consumers & workers	2.30	2.99	2.29	2.48	3.17	2.35	3.79	3.63	3.99	8.51
Environment & health	0.57	0.48	0.71	0.65	0.95	0.32	0.40	0.39	0.84	0.25
Legal, negotiations, and international relations	28.26	18.65	18.30	18.39	28.68	16.39	18.74	18.47	27.31	13.39
Macroeconomy	8.90	11.06	9.35	9.79	9.83	10.67	11.30	11.23	9.24	10.19
Research and analysis	12.05	6.89	6.72	6.76	7.13	2.89	3.76	3.66	0.84	3.22
Trade and business	42.61	55.69	55.85	55.81	44.06	59.93	57.55	57.82	7.14	53.60
Other	0.72	0.80	0.90	0.87	0.79	0.56	0.97	0.93	43.70	1.18

[a] The sample of 51 research outputs discussed in Chap. 5. Terms (%) represent a percentage share of terms within a category in the number of all terms. Occurrences (%) represent the frequency of occurrence of terms in a category among occurrences of all EKD terms.

When we consider the range of used expert terms, researchers and journalists appear to focus largely on trade and business (over 40% of all terms used) and various aspects of legal proceedings, negotiations, and international relations (over 28% of all terms). The latter category of terms is comparably popular among readers. The widest range of terms used by the readers belong to the "others" category, however, when we consider the frequency with which those uncategorised terms appear in the comments, we observe that their usage is rather sporadic and repetitions are rare. Terms from the "others" category account for only 1.18% of all EKD terms mentioned by the readers. Thus each unique "other" term appears only once or a small number of times in the whole corpus of readers' posts. Although the readers seem to utilise a comparably narrow range of trade and business-related terms, those issues constitute a topic of over half of the overall "expert content" in their posts. As expected, journalists and readers use significantly fewer research-related terms.

We observe some changes in the researchers and journalists' focus over time. As Table 6.8 shows, researchers appear to have increased their interest in the agricultural issues in the period after the Great Recession (increase in the use of associated EKD terms from 3.4% to 5.9%), whereas journalists' interest nearly halved during the same period compared to the years before 2009. Notably, farming and food production were much more popular with the readers—one in ten expert terms used by readers related to an agricultural issue. While consumer and workers' issues seem to have scored lower on the researchers' post-Great Recession on agenda, they seem to have gained more attention from journalists. Although the amount of attention they received was still much lower than the firm-centred issues within the business and trade category.

Looking at the frequencies of terms' usage over the entire sample period, the differences between the expert literature and online articles are relatively small (the research and analysis category being the most pronounced difference). In other words, issues raised by journalists appear to reflect the focus of the expert debate and convey expert arguments. There is some divergence in the priorities of the readers who seem much more concerned with issues relating to agriculture and consumer and workers' welfare and less interested in legal or international relations aspects. Thus, readers are more preoccupied with issues that affect them directly and the potential consequences of FTAs on their lives, which could be considered a rational approach.

Overall, there might be a disconnect between the issues and arguments raised by journalists and researchers and those of importance to the readers representing the general public. Although online articles seem to do a good job of reflecting the focal points of the expert debate, they neglect some key issues that are important to the public. All three groups tend to marginalise the impact of the trade deals on environmental and health aspects—only a fraction of a per cent of the EKD terms appearing in the texts pertain to those issues—a rather disappointing result given the climate challenges of the twenty-first century. In the next section, we consider the sentiment and emotional load of the online articles and readers' comments and how they relate to the content of expert knowledge.

6.5 Summarising Remarks

As this chapter shows, trade deals have been attracting an increasing amount of attention in online media in recent years. This observation appears to hold whether we look at the demand side represented by the internet users' demand for information or the supply of articles published in online media. We also present some evidence that those trends are not unique to Poland and are broadly replicated in other countries. Thus, it might be possible that this chapter's findings in the areas of expert knowledge content could be applicable across a larger number of countries and media markets, at least in Europe. Although, such generalisations must be done very cautiously and accompanied by a strong caveat that further study with a broader, international scope is required.

A key lesson from this chapter is that trade negotiations and trade agreements, which are important strategic instruments of geopolitics and economic policy, do not happen in a vacuum and may feed off each other as countries learn from previous experiences. For example, GATT, and later WTO, laid the groundwork for the negotiation and, in some cases, implementation of the other five agreements discussed in this book. Similarly, people's opinions and attitudes towards free trade in general and specific trade deals are likely to be shaped by their knowledge, understanding, and experience of earlier agreements as well as other aspects of international trade. This is further confounded by the chronology of trade-related events as multiple trade deals may be negotiated, signed, and enacted or rejected within relatively short periods of time—2016 and 2017 are very good examples of that. We show that such periods are marked by heated debates among experts, journalists, politicians, and regular people and the views or sentiment towards one FTA may be closely linked to an individual's perception of other FTAs. Those linkages might be stronger when such events are in close temporal proximity.

We observe that journalists tend to base their articles on some degree of expert knowledge measured by the occurrence and frequency of terms typically found in the academic and expert literature on free trade. Furthermore, online articles seem to reflect the positive sentiment towards free trade found in academic experts' writings. This could be considered as a sign that a better understanding of trade issues leads to higher openness and acceptance of FTAs. In contrast, most comments posted by readers below articles do not include any elements of expert knowledge. This is not to say that the comments do not bring any merit or value to the debate. Some of them contain well-informed and thoroughly considered opinions and contribute critical arguments. Nonetheless, the rule seems to be that the more readers an outlet attracts, the more heated the debate in the comments section gets, but at the same time, the share of merit-driven comments drops.

References

Gawronska-Nowak, B., Beck, K., & Valdivieso, P. (2019). Expert knowledge status quoin the internet provided public debate on free trade agreements. Meta analysis of Polish literature. Economics and Sociology, 12(1), 248–261.

IBIMS, Instytut Badań Internetu i Mediów Społecznosć iowych (Institute for Study of Internet and Social Media). (2021). Skad̨ Polacy czerpią informacje? Raport IBIMS i IBRIS. Published on 24 January 2021 at http://ibims.pl/skad-polacy-czerpia-informacje-o-polsce-i-swiecie-raport-ibims-i-ibris/.

Kasiak, Mateusz (2015). Artykuł publicystyczny w świadomości genologicznej dziennikarzy prasowych. Studia Medioznawcze, 63(4), 83-94.

Kasiak, Mateusz (2016). Artykuł publicystyczny w prasie i w internecie. Analiza porównawcza. Rocznik Bibliologiczno-Prasoznawczy 8(19).

Kieraś, Witold, Marcin Woliński (2017). Morfeusz 2—analizator i generator fleksyjny dla języka polskiego. Język Polski, XCVII(1):75–83.

Kula, Agnieszka (2013). O pewnych zasadach sztuki publicystycznej w prasie opiniotwórczej: temporalność i argumentacyjność.

Kula, Agnieszka (2014). Artykuł publicystyczny w tygodnikach społeczno-politycznych. O kilku dualizmach. Oblicza Komunikacji, 6, 47-59.

Morris, Chris (2019). Brexit: What is the 'no deal' WTO option?, BBC News, 29 July 2019, URL: https://www.bbc.co.uk/news/uk-45112872

Shiller, Robert J. (2019). Narrative economics: How stories go viral and drive major economic events. Princeton University Press.

Woliński, Marcin (2014). Morfeusz reloaded. In Nicoletta Calzolari, Khalid Choukri, Thierry Declerck, Hrafn Loftsson, Bente Maegaard, Joseph Mariani, Asuncion Moreno, Jan Odijk, and Stelios Piperidis, editors, Proceedings of the Ninth International Conference on Language Resources and Evaluation, LREC 2014, pages 1106–1111, Reykjavík, Iceland, 2014.

CHAPTER 7

Sentiment and Emotions in the Popular FTA Discourse

Abstract This chapter uses natural language processing tools to analyse the sentiment and emotions contained in online news articles and readers' comments. We argue that the emotional charge conveyed in the media coverage may strongly resonate in the social perception. We also explore the polarising narratives present in the free trade debate and consider the debate surrounding CETA as a mini-case study to capture the polarising narratives. We suggest that the emotional charge found in comments could offer an avenue for measuring the public attitude towards free trade. The online comments are capable of engaging relatively large numbers of individuals, give them a forum to voice their opinions, ask questions, and express expectations, and as such have the potential to become a valuable conduit for a public discussion within a safe and non-exclusive space.

Keywords Sentiment analysis • Emotions • Polarisation • CETA • Wheel of emotions

We perform the analysis of the sentiment and emotions contained in the online texts using two digital tools developed and made available under the umbrella of the Common Language Resources and Technology

B. Gawrońska-Nowak et al., *Trade Wins or Trade Wars*,
https://doi.org/10.1007/978-3-030-76997-0_7

Infrastructure (CLARIN-PL).[1] The primary resource we use in this chapter is the highly versatile Literary Exploration Machine or LEM[2] (Maryl et al. 2017), which has been specifically built for Polish and accounts for the language's high level of inflexion, rich morphology, and weakly constrained word order in sentences. LEM's appeal and usability come from combining several tools into a single package, allowing it to perform multiple types of natural language analysis (see Maryl et al. 2017). We utilise the sentiment analysis function, which is based on the bag-of-words approach and counts terms within each document that are associated with one of the two characteristics: (i) positive, neutral, or negative sentiment (polarisation) and (ii) emotional load. These two types of results are considered in turns in the remainder of this chapter section.

Additionally, we use an alternative tool, MultiEmo, to confirm the robustness of our results from the analysis of emotions contained in the readers' comments.[3] MultiEmo (Kocoń et al. 2021) builds on the earlier work of Kocoń et al. (2019) and Kanclerz et al. (2020) and explores the polarisation of sentiment contained in text on the sentence and document levels. Since it has been trained on consumer reviews that tend to be rather short texts, not very dissimilar to our readers' comments, we use MultiEmo only to analyse the opinions expressed by readers.

The main characteristics of the Polish online media coverage of FTAs have been described in the previous chapter. We know that there is no shortage of expert content in relation to which the emotional content would be overwhelming. That has been spotted in the quantitative analysis. However, it is not only the quantity that matters. The emotional charge conveyed in the media coverage may strongly resonate in the social perception. Instead of numerical superiority, one can bet on its polarisation power.

It seems that the effectiveness of polarising narratives depends on their good embedding in the so-called local context. As Permanyer (2012, p. 47) points out, "*the levels of social polarisation/social tension is the extent to which individuals feel involved and identified with the group to which they*

[1] CLARIN-PL (https://clarin-pl.eu/) is a section of the pan-European research project aiming at creation and development of electronic language tools and resources for natural language processing, aiding researchers in humanities and social sciences in the analysis of large collections of texts in Polish.

[2] Available at https://ws.clarin-pl.eu/lem.shtml.

[3] We are thankful to Jan Kocoń and Bartłomiej Bojanowski for their goodwill and generous assistance in deploying MultiEmo to analyse our corpus of texts.

belong. This feeling of involvement with one's group will be referred as radicalism degree." Thus, polarising narratives should appropriately be "imbued" with some values and symbols that would trigger both a sense of far-reaching identification and the rejection of indifferent attitudes in favour of committed attitudes, so they must be easily consumable within a given culture code. The polarising narratives' attractiveness does not depend only on the hermetic, country, or local-specific symbolic messages. After all, these narratives' essence refers to human emotions, which (regardless of cultural factors) are quite universal.

In the Polish content that we have examined, it is visible how much attention has been paid to CETA recently, the FTA representing a new generation of trade deals. The novelty of CETA provisions, the drastic differences between the external conditions that prevailed during its negotiations, and its signing make CETA a fascinating case study. By studying this case, we attempt to capture the polarising narratives. We also want to see if their polarising power had any effect on the content of the comments.

7.1 Polarisation of Sentiment

We begin by scrutinising the polarisation of sentiment contained in our corpus of data. In other words, we determine whether each article and reader's comment expresses a positive, negative, or neutral attitude towards FTAs. For each item, LEM returns the numbers of words indicating one of the three sentiments. We use this information to calculate polarisation scores that measure a percentage share of words linked to either positive or negative attitude within all sentiment-tagged words found in the analysed item of text. Mathematically, this can be written as:

$$Positive\ score = \frac{Number\ of\ positive\ words}{All\ sentiment\ tagged\ words} \times 100$$

and

$$Negative\ score = -\frac{Number\ of\ negative\ words}{All\ sentiment\ tagged\ words} \times 100,$$

where *All sentiment-tagged words* is a sum of the numbers of words with positive, negative, and neutral sentiment present in an individual article or reader's comment. When calculating the *Negative score* we add a negative algebraic sign into the formula ("-") to ensure that its value sign is opposite to that of the *Positive score*.

The overwhelming majority of texts in our corpus have non-zero values of the positive and negative scores simultaneously, which means that they contain a mixture of terms indicating both positive and negative attitudes. Thus, to establish whether an analysed article or comment is overall favourable towards or against FTAs, we calculate the *Overall sentiment score* as:

$$Overall\ sentiment\ score = Positive\ score + Negative\ score.$$

Figure 7.1 presents the average values of the positive, negative, and overall polarisation (sentiment) scores for the online articles and readers' comments and their breakdown by FTAs and media outlets. Panels a and c indicate that online articles tend to be mostly neutral in their assessment of FTAs as, on average, over 90% of sentiment-tagged words appear to be of neutral sentiment according to the LEM results. Potentially, this could be seen as evidence of journalistic neutrality and objectivity and a focus on informing readers rather than imposing opinions. Nonetheless, the articles are not completely neutral as they appear to convey a weakly positive attitude towards free trade, irrespective of the FTA in question and media outlet. The average positive polarisation score contained in their texts is just above 5%, whereas the negative score is approximately -3% (Panel a, bar *All*).

When we look at journalists' attitudes towards individual trade deals in Panel a of Fig. 7.1, we observe that the differences in positive attitudes (blue bars) across FTAs are rather marginal, but there is more variation in the negative sentiment (red bars). CEFTA appears to attract the least amount of negative sentiment with the negative score of -2.4%, whereas TPP attracts the most negative sentiment with the negative score at -4.97%. Although the overall sentiment scores appear positive for all seven FTAs, the variations in the negative scores lead to a more diverse distribution of overall attitudes. TTIP, followed closely by CEFTA and CETA, enjoys the most favourable attitude. TPP is on the opposite end of the spectrum with its overall sentiment score much lower than of any other FTA. This "least favoured" deal appears to attract relatively high values of positive and negative sentiment scores—this indicates that attitudes towards TPP are the most polarised. This observation is also reflected in

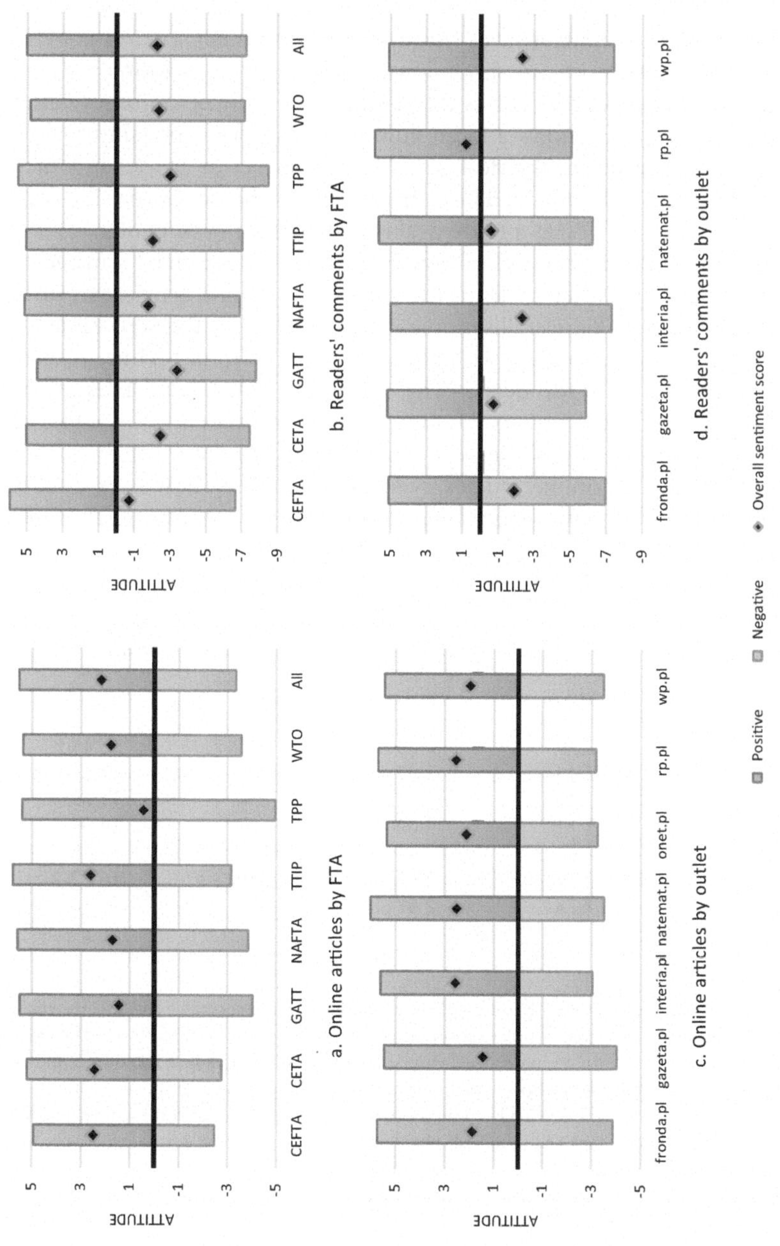

Fig. 7.1 Polarisation of sentiment towards FTAs

Table 7.1 which shows that while on average TPP enjoys the least favourable sentiment in online articles (mean overall sentiment score at 0.44%), it also attracts the most varied opinions. The standard deviation of overall sentiment score towards TPP is 2.93, which is nearly seven times larger than the mean, and shows a large number of articles expressing mainly positive opinions about the deal and a large number of articles in which negative opinions dominate. Thus, there seems to be no journalistic consensus on whether TPP as a trade deal is beneficial or detrimental.

Looking at Panels b and d of Fig. 7.1, we see that readers' sentiments towards FTAs are different from those found in online articles. In both panels, the markers of overall sentiment score are below the zero value for all FTAs and media outlets with the exception of rp.pl.[4] Thus, readers appear sceptical of trade deals.[5] The scepticism towards CEFTA is the weakest, while GATT attracts the most negative sentiment. Although the levels of positive sentiment appear, on average, to be no different from those contained in online articles, readers' comments show over double the amount of negative sentiment. Readers' views are also much more

Table 7.1 Overall sentiment score by FTA

FTA	*Online articles*		*Readers' comments*	
	Mean	*Std. Dev.*	*Mean*	*Std. Dev.*
CEFTA	2.49	2.23	-0.72	17.45
CETA	2.45	2.32	-2.44	17.67
GATT	1.45	2.31	-3.36	14.38
NAFTA	1.71	2.62	-1.77	16.99
TTIP	2.61	2.15	-2.02	16.85
TPP	0.44	2.93	-2.98	16.72
WTO	1.78	2.47	-2.35	16.36

[4] Rp.pl is the only outlet whose readers show a positive overall sentiment towards the trade deals and the smallest degree of polarisation measured by the standard deviation of the overall sentiment scores. This is an interesting observation as, in comparison to the other outlets, rp.pl tends to attract readers who are professionals with higher than average level of education. Thus, individuals who are likely to be more open to international competition and are likely to be better informed (Table 6.7 shows that the usage of expert terms by the readers of rp.pl is one of the highest in the analysed sample).

[5] Using MultiEmo, the previously mentioned alternative tool to analyse the sentiment of readers' comments yields comparable results.

polarised. When we compare the mean values of the overall sentiment scores with their standard deviations in Table 7.1, we observe that the latter are six to 24 times higher. This high degree of overdispersion indicates that large shares of comments contain either strongly positive or strongly negative opinions. While this is likely to be an indicator of lively debates and discussions in readers' forums, it also shows that FTAs are a divisive topic on which there is no consensus among the online readership.

Thus far, we have clear evidence that authors of online articles tend to weakly favour FTAs, whereas their readers' opinions are more polarised and, on average, exhibit a degree of scepticism. But how does this observation link to the indicators of expert knowledge discussed in the previous chapter? Table 7.2 reports coefficients of correlation between the sentiment indicators, the relative frequency of expert terms appearing in analysed texts and their length.

Generally, the correlation coefficients appear modest for online articles and negligible for readers' comments. Thus, there seems to be no link between expert knowledge and the sentiment expressed by readers. In online articles, we observe that the usage of expert terminology is positively linked to the text neutrality. However, the strongest link appears to be between the content of expert terms and the negative sentiment score—pieces with a higher content of expert knowledge tend to exhibit less negative sentiment towards the FTAs. Interestingly, there is no correlation between the expert terms and positive sentiment. These two results put together mean that articles with a greater amount of expert terms are on average more likely to show positive overall sentiment. Another key indication in Table 7.2 is that longer articles appear to be less

Table 7.2 Correlation coefficients between sentiment, the content of expert terms and text length

Sentiment	*Online articles*		*Readers' comments*	
	Percentage of expert words	*Text length (words)*	*Percentage of expert words*	*Text length (words)*
Neutral	0.17	-0.17	0.03	0.05
Positive score	0	0.14	0.03	0.01
Negative score	-0.23	0.11	-0.06	-0.06
Overall sentiment score	0.16	0.02	0.06	0.06

neutral and convey more polarised opinions as both the positive and negative sentiment scores are positively correlated with the number of words.

7.2 Emotions

In this section, we investigate the emotional load of articles written by journalists and comments posted by readers. The Oxford Dictionary defines emotion as "a strong feeling deriving from one's circumstances, mood, or relationships with others".[6] The term's precise meaning may depend on the context but, in general, emotions are associated with feelings, thoughts, behavioural responses and are formed through a cognitive and conscious process initiated by a neurophysiological reaction to significant internal and external events (Cabanac 2002; Schacter et al. 2011; Emory 2018). In the current work, we are interested in understanding the emotional load of the written language used to share information and opinions about the trade deals. We expect emotions, or feelings towards free trade, to play a critical role in influencing and shaping individuals' perception and attitudes towards FTA. In other words, we expect them to be a significant driver of the sentiments and polarisation discussed in the previous section.

LEM, the previously described natural language processing tool, uses the Polish wordnet[7] to identify the emotional connotations of each word in the analysed text. Subsequently, words associated with each emotion category are counted. Following an approach analogous to that in the previous section, for each document, that is an article or a reader's comment, we calculate emotion scores as percentage shares of words associated with a given type of emotion in all words categorised as containing an emotional load:

$$E\ score = \frac{Number\ of\ words\ associated\ with\ emotion\ E}{All\ emotionally\ annotated\ words} \times 100,$$

where *E* stands for one of the following eight types of emotions: joy, sadness, trust (or acceptance), anger, anticipation, disgust, fear, and surprise.

[6] https://www.lexico.com/definition/emotion

[7] *Słowosieć* or the plWordnet is a relational dictionary containing 191,000 words, along with their meanings, word relations, and emotional annotations. It can be accessed via http://plwordnet.pwr.wroc.pl/wordnet/.

This range of emotions is akin to the "wheel of emotions" framework proposed by Plutchik (1988), thus, we use Plutchik's model to systematise our results. Graphically, the model organises eight primary emotions by putting polar opposites on antipodal sides of a "wheel": joy is the opposite of sadness, fear is the opposite of anger, disgust is the opposite of trust, and so on. Figure 7.2 depicts that arrangement along with the average emotion scores calculated for all online articles and all readers' comments. Each of the "radar lines" corresponds to different values of emotion scores with zero or no emotional load in the centre and then rising by 10% increments for each line as we move away from the graph's centre. Thus, the further away the blue or red curve is from the centre, the higher the emotional load present in the articles or comments.

A quick look at Fig. 7.2 reveals that on average online articles are characterised by higher emotion scores than readers' comments. Although, a

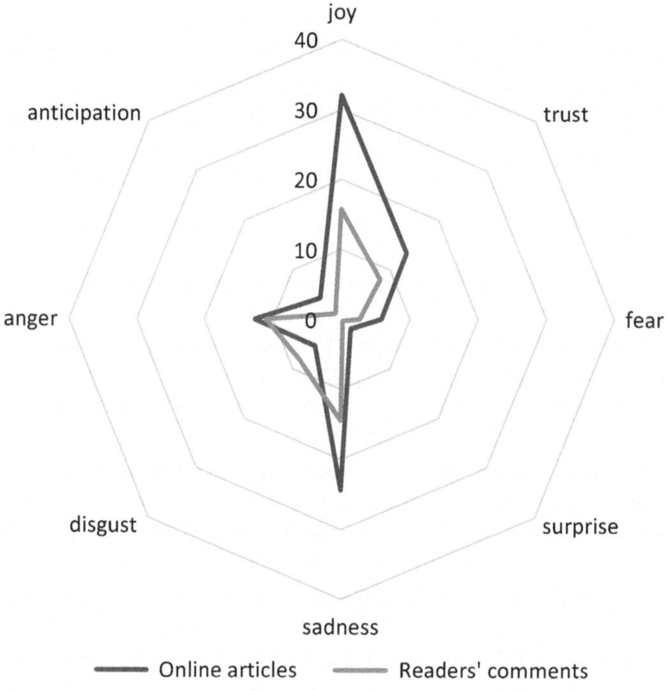

Fig. 7.2 Emotions in all online articles and readers' comments

direct comparison of raw scores between articles and comments is unlikely to be very informative as it is analogous to the proverbial comparison of apples to oranges. The two types of text follow very different patterns, lengths, as well as stylistic and language rules. However, we can compare the relative emotion scores within each text type. When we look at the online articles, we observe that the area encompassed within the blue curve on the "northern" side associated with the positive emotions of trust, joy, and anticipation is larger than the area to the "south" linked to the negative emotions. Thus, we discern that positive emotions towards free trade weakly dominate in the texts written by journalists. This dominance appears to be weak because we also find significant amounts of words indicating negative emotions, especially sadness, but also some non-negligible amounts of anger and fear.

In contrast, the red curve depicting emotion scores for the readers' comments encompasses a larger area in the "south", suggesting that negative emotional connotations prevail in comments raised by readers. As in the case of articles, joy and sadness dominate; however, these two polar opposite emotions appear more balanced in readers' comments, and both achieve emotion scores of 15%. While journalists scored high on trust and expressed little disgust, both emotions feature equally strongly in readers' posts (emotion scores of 8%). Another relatively prominent feeling which pulls the readers' emotions to the negative territory is anger (emotion score of 11%), which appears four times "stronger" than its polar opposite of fear.

Words associated with anticipation and surprise are the least frequent. Such a result should be expected of journalists whose role is to be informed and inform. As we have shown in Chap. 6, the online articles do a relatively good job of reflecting expert knowledge, which suggests that journalists remain in sync with the latest facts and advances in the world of free trade. Thus, they are less likely to perceive developments linked to FTAs as unexpected, unanticipated, or surprising. They are also likely to avoid conveying such feelings in their articles to ensure their writing appears well informed and based on cautious, deliberate arguments and analysis. Proportionately, readers exhibit even lower levels of anticipation and surprise, which on the one hand could suggest a lack of interest. However, on the other hand, spending time and effort to open an online article, familiarise oneself with its content and then post a comment indicates a non-negligible amount of interest in the topic. Thus, the result is not obvious. The low score for anticipation combined with the low level of fear could suggest that they do not feel directly affected by FTAs. The very low surprise score (0.36%—the lowest of all emotions) might imply knowledge of or familiarity with related developments, but as the previous section showed, on average we observe very little or no expert knowledge in readers' comments. A possible explanation behind the low levels of anticipation and surprise could be a contemptuous or "know it all" attitude whereby the discussion forum is dominated by individuals with strong views and opinions in a wide range of topics but no support in factual knowledge. This is a strong assertion which at this stage can be neither ruled out nor confirmed.

In Table 7.3 we present the correlation coefficients between the eight emotions, sentiments, and the indicator of the presence of expert knowledge in online articles and readers' comments. The right-most column appears to confirm the lack of links between readers' emotions and subject knowledge. Although relatively stronger, those links remain at most moderate in the online articles. A greater presence of expert terms in articles is associated with greater levels of positive emotions such as joy, trust, and anticipation. At the same time, we observe that more frequent references to the expert vocabulary, and presumably a better understanding of the international trade issues, may dampen the negative emotions of disgust, fear, and anger.

The correlation coefficients between emotion scores and the measures of sentiment show anticipated signs. In both, online articles and readers' comments, positive emotions seem to translate to positive overall sentiment, and higher levels of negative emotions correlate with overall unfavourable sentiment towards FTAs.

To complete our analysis in the current section, in Figs. 7.3 and 7.4 we show the results for emotion scores on the individual FTA and media outlet levels, respectively. Generally, the figures mirror the image presented in Fig. 7.2 and the results discussed above. We do not see any significant variations in the emotion loads in readers' comments across the seven FTAs. In each case, the negative emotions appear to exceed the positive ones slightly. The emotions contained in online articles remain consistently positive, with joy being the dominant emotion. Nevertheless, there is one exception: in the case of TPP, joy appears narrowly overtaken by sadness, and the overall emotions mix is likely to be negative.

When we consider the emotions by media outlets, we see that the graphs maintain their distinctive pattern of concentration to the north-east and the south-west. There are no notable differences in the emotions

Table 7.3 Correlation between emotions, sentiment, and expert knowledge

Emotion	*Online articles*				*Readers' comments*			
	Sentiment			*Percentage of EKD words*	*Sentiment*			*Percentage of EKD words*
	Positive	*Negative*	*Overall sentiment*		*Positive*	*Negative*	*Overall sentiment*	
Joy	0.38	-0.62	0.70	0.16	0.50	-0.15	0.41	0.10
Trust	0.38	-0.42	0.56	0.11	0.43	-0.13	0.35	0.07
Fear	-0.17	0.42	-0.41	-0.19	-0.04	0.23	-0.20	0.01
Surprise	-0.03	-0.19	0.11	0.10	0.00	0.04	-0.03	0.02
Sadness	-0.37	0.54	-0.64	-0.05	-0.09	0.38	-0.34	0.02
Disgust	-0.15	0.41	-0.39	-0.28	-0.10	0.49	-0.43	0.01
Anger	-0.36	0.54	-0.63	-0.13	-0.11	0.52	-0.46	-0.02
Anticipation	0.04	-0.33	0.26	0.16	0.16	-0.05	0.13	0.02

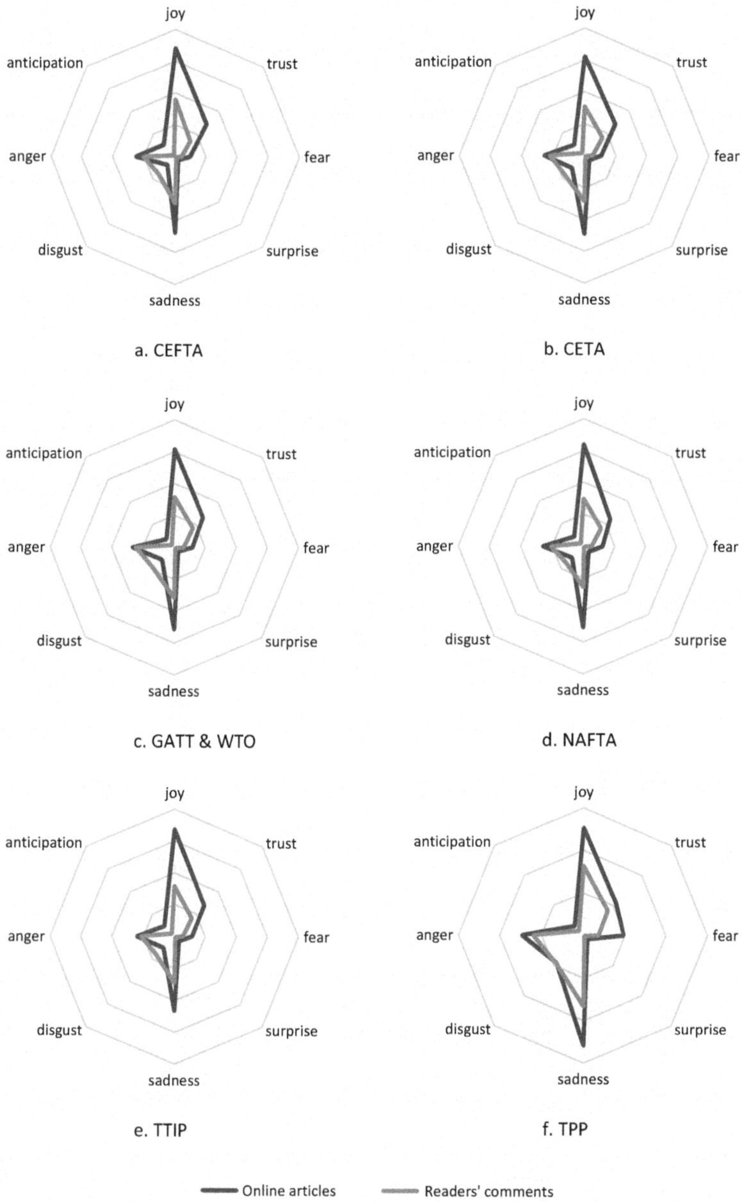

Fig. 7.3 Emotions by FTAs

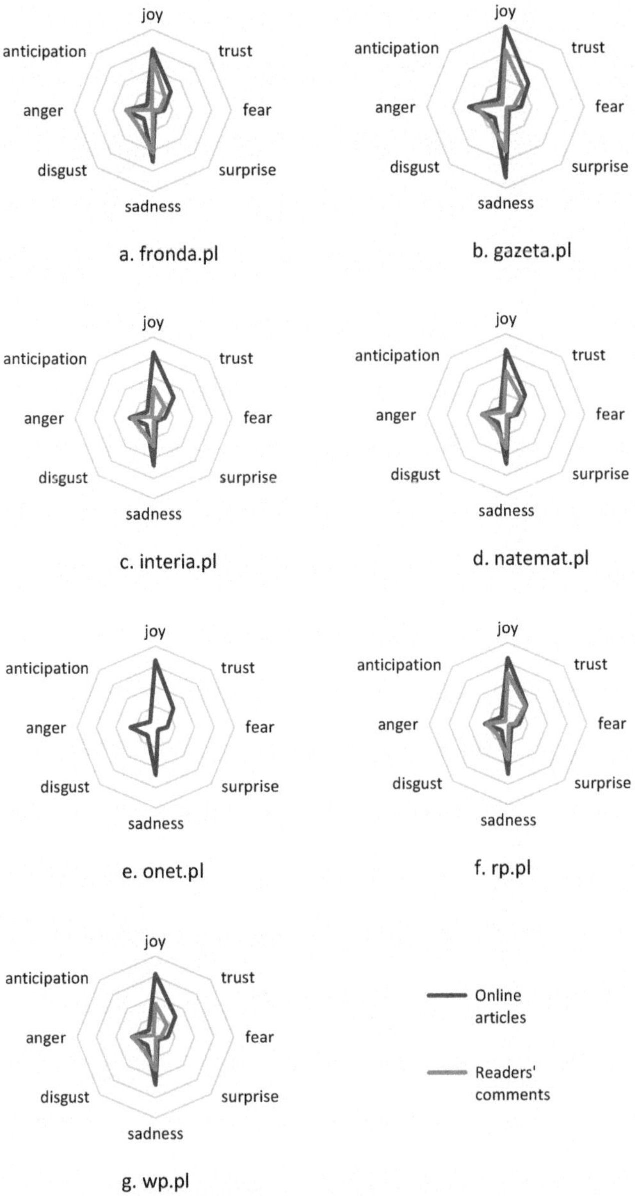

Fig. 7.4 Emotions by media outlet

conveyed in online articles across the outlets. Thus, whether we look at a mainstream, a right-, or a left-leaning portal, journalists appear to express a mainly positive mixture of emotions. We observe some more variation in readers' posts. Comments to articles on the right-leaning fronda.pl exhibit the highest levels of almost all emotions, including joy (25.4%).

Similarly, the content on the left-leaning natemat.pl also shows above-average emotion scores, although relatively smaller than fronda.pl. As these two portals attract readership with polar opposite views, they also appear to channel polar opposite emotions. The right-leaning fronda.pl records the highest emotion scores for anger (13.2%) and disgust (10.7%), whereas its left-leaning counterpart, natemat.pl, leads in fear (3.6%) and trust (10.9%). When we turn to rp.pl, which attracts mostly professionals with higher education levels, we see that its readers appear to be as positive about FTAs as the journalists are. This should not be a surprise since the outlet's readership is the only group of readers whose overall sentiment towards FTAs is positive.

7.3 Qualitative Analysis: Internet Debate on CETA Case Study

In this section, we conduct a qualitative analysis of internet content. We look through all the articles devoted to CETA and posted on: fronda, gazeta.pl, interia, natemat, onet, and rp. We find 32 of them exceptionally appealing and illustrative as transmission sources of the polarising narratives. We use these 32 articles as our reference material to identify three vital polarising narratives: "*Red Herring*", "*Messiah 2.0*", and "*Antiglobalism, anticorporationism, fatigue neoliberalism*". Moreover, we analyse all comments that belong to these articles.

The content of the CETA comments does not look like identical mirror images of the narratives present in the articles. However, there are visible connections between article and comment narratives that can be treated as some manifestation of elite cueing. In the populism period, when the elite, especially the decision-makers, listen carefully to the people's voice, one cannot be sure who the sender of the message is and who the recipient is, what the "feedback" mechanism looks like from the inside. Be it the elite succumbing to the "masses" or the "masses" to the elites. One thing is sure, the similarities between the narrative in the articles and the narrative in the comments are noticeable.

7.3.1 *Polarising Narratives in the Articles*

"Red herring"

According to this narrative, an issue as crucial as CETA is intentionally ignored in public debate. Instead of a discussion on CETA, other topics that may be thrilling to the public opinion, such as abortion or partnerships, were raised. The "red herring" narrators offer a vision of reality whereby some undefined "backseat drivers" navigate the public opinion towards massive deception. Such a narrative fits in well with the conspiracy theories.

While following the "red herring" narrative, the right-wing media blame other media for their "*hysterical tone*" and campaigns that "*are distracting for the public opinion*". It seems that the reference to the hysterical tone of the liberal media concerning the issue of abortion and partnerships is not only intended to emphasise the importance of the overlooked issues (such as CETA) but also (or even above all) to discredit the importance of abortion or partnerships as major social problems. Interestingly, the term "*red herring*" is also used in some liberal and leftist media to refer to the anti-abortion policy.[8] At the end of the day, both right-wing and left-wing media readily accuse the government of manipulating public attention to avoid discussing various political scandals such as "Minister Misiewicz's antics[9]" and nepotism.

(1) These are some exemplifications of this narrative: "*Such matters as partnerships, abortion and IVF are brought to light by the government to distract public opinion from other significant issues", says Paweł Kukiz broadcasting in the TVN24 program "Kropka nad i".*

[8] The majority of the articles were posted not later than in 2017. It was before the second wave of the so-called black protests caused by a Constitutional Court ruling on radical tightening of the abortion law.

[9] After the election victory of Law and Justice in 2015, Bartłomiej Misiewicz became the head of the political cabinet and the press spokesman of the Ministry of National Defense. He also became a political assistant to Antoni Macierewicz (Minister of National Defense). On 28 January 2019, he was detained by the Central Anticorruption Bureau. Five other people were arrested with him. They were accused of, among other things, invocation of influence and profit-taking from it. Misiewicz was temporarily arrested for three months. Then his detention was extended for another two months. He was released in June 2019 after paying a bail of 100,000 PLN.

"Nothing is said about re-privatisation, Misiewicz and signing CETA", added the politician.

(2) *Minister Kowalczyk on CETA: "We do not want to worsen the Polish situation in the hysteria surrounding the anti-abortion law, we all miss the discussion about CETA, although the topic raises a lot of controversies". Minister Henryk Kowalczyk was a guest of the "Political Quarter" programme on TVP 1.*

(3) *Luiza Dołęgowska, Fronda.pl: Do you think that there is a visible trend related to pointing out by the media to matters of little importance and omitting essential matters—that is, 'fashionable' publicising the case of Mr Misiewicz, and ignoring or omitting matters more important to citizens (help for families, profits of companies that were unprofitable years, rescue the industry)?*

Piotr Strzembosz, Right of the Republic of Poland: "I agree that the media are looking for marginal issues that serve them to whip their disliked parties and disliked politicians. The plain truth is that PiS that promotes such a politician like Misiewicz, gives hostile media an easy excuse to attack the party. The issue of the "hysterical narrative" you raised is, unfortunately, the norm in the Polish media. We are looking forward to in-depth analyses in the opinion-forming media on foreign policy or internal, economic and social affairs, because the debate is dominated by the eternal struggle of two political camps for necessary, but not the most critical issues. Very often, the so-called news television stations bring together representatives of two opposing political formations to ask them about essentially marginal issues—a controversial statement, a scandal, or moral issues. And the real political and economic interests of Poland, or the threats to our country, lie in the CETA agreement, which was concealed by the media. The issue of the current authorities' consent to the absorption of European "norms" concerning, for example, gender or fundamental human rights, which should include human life from the moment of conception, is also omitted."

There seems to be a hidden desire in this narrative to discredit, delegitimise, and take away the adversary's respect. According to this narrative, the opponents do not take up truly essential topics; they deal with some "*red herrings*" only, use various tricks and manipulations. In conclusion, they do not deserve real attention and subjectivity. The topic of CETA—although mentioned many times in this context—does not convey any substantive message. It serves more as a counterpoint. It is to contrast with the "*unimportant*" themes. As a severe subject of "*no discussion*", it is mainly presented as a type of threat. It helps writers build a hierarchy of apparent and real threats. CETA is thus becoming a rhetorically useful tool to polarise the discussion. This polarisation is based on the black and one division into important and unimportant matters, but also—by assigning emotional labels ("*hysterical narration*")—divides the subjects of discussion and discussants into emotional (i.e. unreliable, unstable, irrational) and substantive (trustworthy, stable, rational).

"Messiah 2.0"

This is a strong message coming primarily from the government representatives that may sometimes even have quite contradictory or unclear opinions on the impact of CETA on the Polish economy, but they usually present the superpower vision of Poland quite consistently. This vision consists of a mixture of a sense of superiority ("*Canada is a small economy*"—compared to Poland, implicitly) and inferiority complex ("*We are being ridiculed, people* [abroad] *poke fun at us*") or fears ("*we survived the war and communism. That is the truth. And now, we are being bought out, they* [the West] *are better off*").[10]

These are some exemplifications of this narrative:

(1) *"Waszczykowski believes that the agreement with Canada should be considered on three levels: geopolitical, economic and legal."*
(2) *"In the case of the geopolitical plane, he* [Waszczykowski[11]] *assessed that the agreement 'seems to be beneficial because it may create a large area of geopolitical cooperation'. He reckoned that if the EU also signed a free trade agreement with the United States, 'it would be such an economic NATO'. 'And we know that world economies are competing with each other, with China and with others', added the head of the Ministry of Foreign Affairs. According to him, 'on the geopolitical level, it is a positive agreement'."*
(3) *"'When it comes to the economic level, it seems neutral, because* ***the Canadian economy is not a big economy.*** *For example, as Poland,*

[10] The quotations come from a qualitative study conducted in Poland in late 2017 and analysed in the article by Konieczna-Sałamatin and Sawicka (2020), p. 8.

[11] Former Minister of Foreign Affairs (affiliated with PIS, Law and Justice, the ruling party).

we trade with Canada at a level below USD 4 billion'—said Waszczykowski."

(4) *"Referring to the legal level, he* [Waszczykowski] *stressed that 'legal systems, dispute resolution and arbitration are very different in Europe, Canada and the United States'."*

Asked for the opinion that signing CETA will open the door for genetically modified food and may be harmful to the Polish market, he replied: "In the case of Canada, not because it is a small economy".

The fears refer to the need to maintain "*our own high standards*" and thus not be subject to foreign (implicitly harmful) influences. The key to this narrative is to emphasise the necessity "*to have an influence on what is going on there*", for example: "*We want one of the judges appointed by the EU to be a person designated by our country*". Quite common (regardless of the writers' ideological inclinations) is the belief in the excellent quality of Polish food and the necessity to protect this quality. This is clearly compensation for the above-described inferiority complex.

(1) *"Poland did not raise any objections and saw no grounds to suspend the signing of this agreement, as do most of the countries, except Belgium, Bulgaria and Romania", said Jerzy Kwieciński. "For us, the key issue is that we have an influence on what is going on there", said the deputy minister. "We want one of the judges appointed by the EU to be a person designated by our country", he added.*

(2) *According to Młodzież Wszechpolska (the All-Polish Youth) food production will become more expensive and the food itself will be of lower quality. The demonstrators explained that after the implementation of the agreement, Polish agriculture would suffer, first of all, because cheap, modified food will flood Polish stores and agricultural production will no longer be profitable for farmers.*

(3) *So who can CETA be a problem for? For the big producers. This type of agreement will require specific changes in the commercial structure. The big ones who work on a 2 and 3% margin will have to look for new areas. Polish food is very attractive. It is an export commodity which is welcome in European markets. Let us imagine that we enter a market twice the size of the European Union!*

Such a narrative brings to mind the reasoning of Erich Fromm on the authoritarian personality. He believed that self-denial and shedding of "I" because of fear and escape from freedom occur in two ways. On the one hand, it may be to merge with "we" through total and extreme obedience. The individual merges with "we" by complete subordination to the authority. On the other hand, getting rid of the "*I*" can be achieved in a somewhat paradoxical way of full control over another, appropriation, objectification, "possession", where again a safe "I" is achieved in some "we".

The authoritarian personality is contained in a specific dialectic of the sadomasochistic character. A distinguishing feature of sadomasochistic individuals is their attitudes towards authority. They admire the authority and would be willing to succumb to it, but at the same time, they would like to be an authority themselves and subjugate others (Fromm, 2008, p. 161). A split personality stretched between being omnipotent and submissive to globalisation, world markets, multilateral agreements, and various groups' interests resonate in this (marked with some authoritarian personality features) narrative.

An equally appealing historic track in the search for the sources of this narrative is the romantic idea of Polish messianism. The idea of messianism in Poland has its roots in the nineteenth century and was expressed first of all in Romantic-era literature. It was connected with the traumatic period of Polish history when the Polish state disappeared for over 100 years (1795–1918). The contemporary version of messianism was borne as a result of various historical events (100 years of lost sovereignty due to Partitions of Poland, severe consequences of both world wars, more than four decades of communism). It was strictly connected to the expectations and that, after unfavourable times for the country, the longed-for period of peace and stabilisation would come. It was a very suggestive vision existing in the Polish minds, which gives a sense of security, hope for a period of happiness. Preserved over the years in art and culture, passed down over many generations, it provided the basis for a specific ideological attitude (see, e.g. Fels 2001). This attitude allows preferring illusion to reality, avoid confrontation with this reality and take responsibility and blame it on someone from the outside, the so-called strangers. Objectively, the historical periods of the Polish state's absence actually made it challenging to develop self-awareness and self-criticism (Grosfeld and Zhuravskaya 2015). It was believed that maintaining identity required idealisation and self-affirmation. Unfortunately, today it is romantic messianism heritage that can largely account for the ease with which Poles succumb to illusions and It may express hostility to groups perceived as responsible for the misfortunes and suffering of the nation—like in the past, our ancestors did it with the partitioning states and other oppressing nations.

The international context's perception seems to be primarily subordinated to this mixture of feelings of superiority and fears, trapped in own image of being specially chosen, anointed for great things and at the same time a victim, wronged by everyone and eternally threatened.

The agreement creates opportunities for Polish processed products. One can point here, for example, the export success of apple juice on the Canadian market. Our food has a chance to appear as ecological. One should agree with the leading thesis of the Polish Chamber of Commerce that Poland is not a lonely island on the economic map of the world.

The statement: "*Poland is not a lonely island on the economic map of the world*" can serve as one example of the perception developments rooted in messianism. An island is used quite perversely, as it sounds somewhat abstract and exotic in relation to Poland's geographical conditions. Hence, we have a symbolic reference to something extraordinary and unique (an island that is not an island). Although there is a denial that we are not lonely and isolated in this statement, but a specific selection of words, their symbolic meaning is intensified by the association with some exceptional, unique being on the world map. It also seems significant that the term "island" was introduced to the Polish economic debate by Donald Tusk, who described Poland's position during the global financial crisis of 2008 as the Polish government's prime minister. Pointing to the positive economic growth rates while the rest of the European Union experienced a recession, he used the term "*Poland is a green island*" in recognition of the positive economic performance. It was quickly picked up by the media and disseminated.

Again—though slightly different than in the case of the "*red herring*" narrative—one can get the impression that this "Messiah 2.0" is a polarising narrative. That kind of narrative does not take nuance. Either you accept the whole image or you do not, you can only be in this imaginary or entirely out of it. A rationalisation is useless here as it would require confronting the illusion with reality, which is excluded *ex definitione*.

"Antiglobalism, anticorporationism, fatigue neoliberalism"

This narrative seems to be relatively consistent with the universal message opposing large international corporations' influence, stigmatising capitalism, and globalisation. It combines opposition to GM food and suspicion of any agreements concluded "over the heads of lay citizens" favouring the wealthy elite's interests. In a milder version, it is supported by the experts who point out the harmful effects of trade agreements resulting in job losses, and they postulate the introduction of policies that would mitigate these adverse effects.

Within this narrative, the key actors who take the floor can be identified with both the right side of the Polish political scene and its left side, for example Młodzież Wszechpolska (the All-Polish Youth), Ruch Kukiz 15 (the Kukiz Movement' 15), or Akcja Demokracja (the Democracy Action Foundation). They sound quite similar:

(1) *"According to Młodzież Wszechpolska (the All-Polish Youth), food production will become more expensive, and the food itself will be of lower quality. The demonstrators explained that after the agreement's implementation, Polish agriculture would suffer because cheap, modified food will flood Polish stores and agricultural production will no longer be profitable for farmers. The CETA agreement provides for lifting almost all customs duties and non-tariff barriers and the liberalisation of trade in services between the European Union and Canada. It also provides for high compensation from countries that break the provisions of the agreement. Its implementation will be supervised by transnational corporations employing lawyers who will be able to sue nation-states in the event of any breach of the provisions of this agreement."*

(2) *"The organisation of the protest was dealt with by the Akcja Demokracja (the Democracy Action Foundation), supported by trade unions, Partia Razem (the Together Party), SLD (the Democratic Left Alliance) and Ruch Kukiz 15 (the Kukiz Movement '15). The representative of the protest organisation, Piotr Trzaskowski, argued that today's actions were not an objection to corporations' omnipotence."*

"The government claims that the arbitration tribunals included in TTIP and CETA pay off in Poland. It is a brazen twisting everything round. There are independent courts of law in resolving disputes, not suspicious institutions created under the dictates of big business", said Adrian Zandberg before the demonstration began. People gathered not only in Warsaw, with the slogans: "CETA to the toilet" ("CETA do klozeta"), "Eat whatever you want, but not CETA" ("Jedzta co chceta, byle nie CETA") or simply "STOP CETA".

There are many (negative) references to ACTA and TTIP in the statements. ISDS raises a lot of controversy and aversion. More radical voices are supported by experts' opinions who express similar views in a more balanced way.

(1) "*ACTA twins conceived behind closed doors. CETA or the Comprehensive Economic and Trade Agreement is an international agreement between the European Union and Canada countries. The agreement was created on the assumption that its predecessor, ACTA, would be adopted.*"
(2) "*It should be emphasised that the CETA agreement, like the TTIP agreement or the TPP agreement, are all-inclusive agreements. There, the lifting of typically trade barriers in the form of customs duties is a marginal one", noted Oręziak. In her opinion, according to CETA, anything could be considered a trade barrier and could constitute a restriction in market access.*

"Supporters of the CETA agreement claim that these are unjustified fears because when Poland entered the European Union, it was also said that our market would be flooded. Only that the great opening of the Polish market to competition from goods and services from other European Union countries was accompanied and continues by the generous cohesion policy, however, this is a considerable amount of money that has been flowing for several years, and we hope it will continue to flow. (...) This is some part of the compensation for an opening", she pointed out. "And what is there (in CETA and TTIP—PAP) for this market opening? What in exchange?" she asked. "There is no such compensation for the social costs of this agreement." "Free trade also comes with a price. Just as there is no free lunch, there is no free trade. Someone has to pay for it", added Oręziak.

This type of narrative is quite obviously similar to CETA's widespread criticism by various NGOs, alter- and anti-globalists from all over the world. It is a universal narrative in its message. It is anti-elitist, anti-corporate, and emphasises the "common people" perspective. Paradoxically, it is quite an elite narrative at the same time, in the sense that, compared to the other distinguished narratives, it is probably most visibly supported by experts and authorities' statements.

7.3.2 *Polarisation in Comments on CETA*

Most of the analysed opinions expressed in the CETA comments are quite emotional, which seems to be rather a natural feature of most internet forum discussion threads. In our CETA-related debate case, those who write them demonstrate their lack of trust (in the Polish government, in foreign corporations, in the EU, in foreign countries, in the outside world). Distrust takes the form of suspicion of trade deals (CETA and TTIP) that were made: "*at the expense of the ordinary people*", that "*serves the interests of multinational corporations*". In particular, CETA is perceived as the tricky backdoor (Trojan horse) to the food imported from the US, that is GMO food. The government and other Polish politicians are blamed for "*the betrayal of the Polish raison d'etat*". In the formulations used, the motif of the fictitious, ineffective state", that is "*cardboard state*", "*theoretical state*" appears.

(1) "*The signing of the CETA and TTIP agreement is a BETRAYAL of the Polish raison d'etat, the Polish economy, Polish agriculture, the Polish Constitution and the Polish Nation* !!!"
(2) "*And Poland is sold, TTIP comes, and Poland will not be even a theoretical state anymore.*"

The ISDS seems to be the leading theme in this distrust-streaked popular narrative. It is known that the ISDS was highly controversial. The law that allows foreign private investors to sue the state must provoke mixed reactions, and especially among supporters and propagators of the "Messiah 2.0" narrative should be the so-called grist to the mill. It is worth noting that under CETA, completely different provisions of ISDS were adopted as a result of various objections and criticisms about how ISDS had been adopted and proposed earlier (e.g. in TTIP draft). However, it seems that the emotional load of the "Messiah 2.0" narrative is so strong that even the new solutions adopted in CETA, aimed at objectification and transparency of arbitration proceedings, are also perceived at least with suspicion and arouse fears and concerns. These fears are expressed in a more or less intellectually sophisticated way:

(1) "*Power, including judicial power, is a form of rule over someone. For the time being, the judiciary is exercised by the citizens of the EU by their own courts, because they are democratic republics, and thus they*

themselves exercise judicial power over themselves. These 'new courts' of CETA are power over Polish citizens exercised not by those citizens over themselves, but by a power outside the Polish sovereign. It is a foreign power that is deceitfully imposed on us, secretly, under the guise of CETA, hidden in CETA, which as an agreement is supposed to be a free trade agreement, but is in fact extortion of consent to surrender to power outside the sovereign of a given EU Member State."

(2) *"CETA and TTIP are agreements that benefit only multinational corporations. The dispute resolution mechanism between the state and the corporation, i.e. ISDS, will force us to adapt the regulations to the needs of the corporation, or we will have to pay huge compensations."*

On the other hand, it seems that most of the discussants do distinguish CETA from TTIP and somehow graduate the "scale of the threat" associated with these deals. This can be inferred from the "frame" which says that CETA is the gateway to TTIP, that it is a kind of bypassing of trade barriers for American products which, thanks to CETA, can freely enter Poland and Europe unmarked. In this narrative, American products are synonymous with GMO food and evoke a great sense of danger and aversion among the discussants. So—to sum up—CETA and Canadian products in themselves, if they were not that secret passage to American food, would not arouse such dislike.

The peculiar architecture of fear, including the various levels of fears expressed in the comments, activates very primal, existential fears:

"Let us defend ourselves and organise protests, because this is about our life, about our existence and our children. Down with CETA and TTIP!"

The references to Russia seem quite interesting in the context of how the lay commentators perceive the external environment of their universe. Russia's image in the average Pole's eyes does not seem too friendly (Sygnowski and Mazurkiewicz 2020, 8–9). Difficult historical experiences, in which Russia played the role of an occupant of Polish lands, certainly significantly influence this, but no less important are more recent events that began in 2014 when Russia went into an open military conflict with Ukraine. It is also known that today there are not many good practices of bilateral cooperation that could help replace old ideas about oneself with new ones (as it was primarily achieved in relations between Poland and Germany). This is especially difficult after the annexation of Crimea in 2014, which was generally supported by the Russian society (Sherlock 2020; Biersack and Lear 2014). Meanwhile, threats perceived today as global and coming from the outside—such as those, according to commentators CETA- or TTIP-related—tame other and older fears. In this light, Russia appears more like a recognised, and perhaps—in this connection—a familiar companion in general misery, unwanted but less alien than other jeopardies.

(1) "*After CETA and TTIP—we will cry for the Russian "occupier"*.
(2) "*Macierewicz the Russophobe has traded the support of* CETA *and* TTIP *for the cardboard PATRIOTS*!"

One can even get the cautious impression that in these statements there is a particular sentiment behind the old world and old relationships in which Russia played some "evil but real, valuable role"—unlike the "*cardboard Patriots*", which sounds unreal and invaluable, and is a reference to the surface-to-air missile (SAM) system, used by the United States Army, the current allies of Poland. These potentially resentful references to Russia (opposite to the American food, American investors, and big American corporations) are quite remarkable, given the Poles' declared enthusiasm and sympathy for the Americans.[12]

7.4 Summarising Remarks

The three narratives distinguished in the Polish internet discourse on CETA seem to be streaked with anger. It is no coincidence that anger—as opposed to disgust—is recognised as an emotion that can trigger political engagement and activity (Lambert et al. 2019; Scott and Jerit, 2018). All three narratives seem to contain much anger, which is most probably crucial for the narrators to construct their own imaginaries, to support their message, to make it sound strong and unquestionable. In the "*Red Herring*" narrative, anger is aimed at all opponents, all those who think differently from the narrators. Additionally, "the others" are completely discredited as equal participants in public discourse by the narrators. Therefore, at the source of this narrative, one can also see disgust or loathing. Loathing (according to Plutchik's Wheel of Emotions) is treated as a more intense version of disgust. The result is a zero-one world, as in the other two narratives.

[12] https://cbos.pl/EN/publications/reports/2020/031_20.pdf

None of all three described narratives (including neither the "*Messiah 2.0*" narrative nor—even less—the "*Antiglobalism, anticorporationism, fatigue neoliberalism*" narrative), although they have their country-specific cultural references, seem to be the product solely "made in Poland". The anger and disgust that feed all three of these narratives have their universal power. In the messianic vision, disagreement with reality manifests itself in an alternative, exaggerated world to which one must either conform or become its enemy (quite literally). Imaginary greatness is the basis of this universe, which seems quite close to many social groups worldwide. Slogans such as "*make America great again*" and "*let's take back control*" sound very familiar in this universe and harmonise with the "*Messiah 2.0*" core concept very well. The "*Antiglobalism, anticorporationism, fatigue neoliberalism*" is so common—no matter what language it is expressed in—that it could actually happen anywhere on the globe, and it would probably sound the same.

Most of the analysed opinions expressed in the CETA comments are quite emotional, and they follow the key narratives captured in media coverage. The emotional charge found in comments could offer an interesting avenue for measuring the public attitude towards free trade. The online comments sections are capable of engaging relatively large numbers of individuals, give them a forum to voice their opinions, ask questions and express expectations, and as such have the potential to become a valuable conduit for an open and honest public discussion within a safe and non-exclusive space. An appropriately designed and administered commenting facility could be an important tool to bridge the gap in modern polarised societies. However, for this to happen, online media would need to design, implement, and observe clear and objective moderation practices, involve fact-checkers and experts who could reduce the spread of fake news, root out malicious content aimed at causing confusion and disinformation and, generally, steer the debate towards a merit- and fact-based discussion. The open question is who should be responsible for undertaking and monitoring such activities. Profit-driven publishers may have no incentive to engage in such costly to them but socially beneficial practices, they may also lack objectivity. But more importantly, this would raise a whole range of questions related to the freedom of speech and the freedom of expressions and thus should not be done lightly.

References

Biersack, John, and Shannon O Lear. 2014. "The Geopolitics of Russia's Annexation of Crimea : Narratives, Identity, Silences, and Energy." Eurasian Geography and Economics 55 (3). doi: https://doi.org/10.1080/15387216.2014.985241.

Cabanac, M. (2002). What is emotion?. Behavioural processes, 60(2), 69-83.

Emory, Margaret (2018) On Fear, Emotions, and Memory: An Interview with Dr. Joseph LeDoux. BrainWorld, 6 June 2018. Available at: https://brainworld-magazine.com/on-fear-emotions-and-memory-an-interview-with-dr-joseph-ledoux

Fels, Bradley E. 2001. "Polish Messianism 'Redivivus': The Use of Sacrificial Imagery to Gain American Support for Poland during World War II." The Polish Review 46 (2): 195–207. https://www.jstor.org/stable/25779253.

Grosfeld, Irena, and Ekaterina Zhuravskaya. 2015. "Cultural vs. Economic Legacies of Empires: Evidence from the Partition of Poland." Journal of Comparative Economics 43 (1): 55–75. doi:https://doi.org/10.1016/j.jce.2014.11.004.

Kanclerz, Kamil, Piotr Miłkowski, & Jan Kocoń (2020). Cross-lingual deep neural transfer learning in sentiment analysis. Procedia Computer Science, 176, 128-137.

Kocoń, Jan, Piotr Miłkowski & Kamil Kanclerz (2021). MultiEmo: Multilingual, Multilevel, Multidomain Sentiment Analysis Corpus of Consumer Reviews. 2021 Annual Conference of the North American Chapter of the Association for Computational Linguistics, Mexico City, 6—11 June 2021.

Kocoń, Jan, Piotr Miłkowski & Monika Zaśko-Zielińska (2019). Multi-level sentiment analysis of PolEmo 2.0: Extended corpus of multi-domain consumer reviews. In *Proceedings of the 23rd Conference on Computational Natural Language Learning (CoNLL)* (pp. 980-991).

Konieczna-Sałamatin, Joanna, and Maja Sawicka. 2020. "The East of the West, or the West of the East? Attitudes toward the European Union and European Integration in Poland after 2008." East European Politics and Societies: And Cultures, no. June (June): 1–21. doi:https://doi.org/10.1177/0888325420926633.

Lambert, Alan J., Fade R. Eadeh, and Emily J. Hanson. "Anger and its consequences for judgment and behavior: Recent developments in social and political psychology." *Advances in Experimental Social Psychology* 59 (2019): 103-173.

Maryl, M., Piasecki, M., & Walkowiak, T. (2017). Literary Exploration Machine A Web-Based Application for Textual Scholars. In Selected papers from the CLARIN Annual Conference 2017, Budapest, 18–20 September 2017 (No. 147, pp. 128-144). Linköping University Electronic Press.

Plutchik, Robert (1988). The Nature of Emotions: Clinical Implications. In: Clynes M., Panksepp J. (eds) Emotions and Psychopathology. Springer, Boston, MA. doi:https://doi.org/10.1007/978-1-4757-1987-1_1

Schacter, D., Gilbert, D., Wegner, D., & Hood, B. M. (2011). Psychology: European Edition. Macmillan International Higher Education.

Sherlock, Thomas. 2020. "Russian Society and Foreign Policy: Mass and Elite Orientations After Crimea." Problems of Post-Communism 67 (1): 1–23. doi:https://doi.org/10.1080/10758216.2018.1561190.

Sygnowski, Grzegorz, and Łukasz Mazurkiewicz. 2020. "Poland—Russia. Social Diagnosis 2020." Warsaw. http://cprdip.pl/assets/media/Wydawnictwa/Raporty/POLAND_RUSSIA_Social_Diagnosis_2020.pdf.

CHAPTER 8

Media and Populism

Abstract In this chapter, we create a media populism ratio based on Farrand and Carrapico's (2019) key characteristics of populist and technocratic political styles. The self-imposed question, which at the same time constitutes a certain summary of our prior considerations, concerns the role the media might play in shaping the polarisation mechanism. We use the Polish media landscape to highlight some key summarising observations.

Keywords Polarisation and populism • Polish media landscape • Media Populism Ratio

In Chap. 7, we presented the polarising narratives of the free trade discourse on the Polish internet. The interpretation of the narratives' wording corresponds to our quantitative analyses' results indicating a high share of content marked with anger and disgust. By deciphering the so-called local colour encoded in these narratives' DNA, we also drew attention to its universal features. The self-imposed question, which at the same time constitutes a certain summary of our prior considerations, concerns the role the media might play in shaping the polarisation mechanism. Levendusky and Malhotra (2016, p. 296) prove that: "(...) *polarised media coverage causes citizens to view the opposing party less positively*". The results of their work are still unique. The relation between media coverage

B. Gawrońska-Nowak et al., *Trade Wins or Trade Wars*,
https://doi.org/10.1007/978-3-030-76997-0_8

and polarisation processes should be explored and developed as the key research theme. In this chapter, we attempt to throw in our two cents as our investment in that potential growth area.

We create a media populism ratio, which is based on the idea by Farrand and Carrapico (2021), which says that populism is a system of communication that possesses its own (different from the technocratic one) "*logic of argumentation, mode of communication and meaning-making, distinct narratives, with appeals to distinct sources of legitimacy*". We rely on Farrand and Carrapico's key characteristics of populist and technocratic political styles to define our measure.

8.1 Populism's "*Express Yourself*"

As Lonergan and Blyth (2020) observe, economics has become *"angrynomics"*. European politics, like that practised in the United States, has been filled with hostility, distrust, and mutual contempt aimed at constant delegitimisation of the other side. In this context, Poland is just one example of democratic backsliding since the return to power of the PiS (Law and Justice) party in 2015. However, Tworzecki points out (2019, p. 98): "(…) *the puzzle presented by Poland is that it appears to contradict decades of accumulated political science research on transitions to and from democracy in that it lacks any of the major risk factors identified by previous literature, such as persistent economic dysfunction, crippling racial or ethnic divisions, polarising winner-take-all institutions (e.g., presidentialism or single-member-district elections), or pernicious international entanglements (e.g., trade dependence on nondemocracies)*".

The possibility of engaging in even moderate polemics with Tworzecki seems quite tempting. First of all, the problem of income inequality in Poland, as shown by recent studies (Brzezinski and Salach 2020; Brzezinski et al. 2019; Brzeziński 2017), can hardly be assessed as less worrying or different than in other European countries. Despite the relatively short period of wealth accumulation in the period of the market economy after 1989, Poland and Hungary's level of inequality reached those noted in France and Spain (Brzezinski and Salach 2020). Second, without questioning Poland's distinctiveness as a transformative entity, it would be gross negligence to overlook the common influences and similarities underlying social and economic processes in Poland and other European Union countries. Again, referring to the economic reasoning, these numerous interrelations manifest themselves in the form of cycle synchronisation within the EU economy, the strength of mutual EU trade ties, and spillover effects in the EU financial markets. Even if one wanted to abandon the recently criticised economic view of matters, a certain universalism of thinking—including Poland's case—on the subject of social anger, polarisation, and populism still would make sense.

The term "affective polarisation", which originally was used to describe an increased partisan animosity between Democrats and Republicans in the US (Iyengar et al. 2019; Levendusky 2018), can also be applied to European politics. Reiljan (2020) used the Affective Polarisation Index to prove that affective polarisation is present in European party systems, as partisans are often extremely hostile towards competing parties. In a sample of 22 countries surveyed, the most polarised countries appeared to be those in Central-Eastern and Southern Europe. Their levels of affective polarisation were notably higher than in the United States.

Palonen (2009), describing the relationship between polarisation and populism as an interpretative basis for the escalation of these phenomena in Hungary, indicates that polarisation (understood especially as a keynote of political expression) is both a logic and a political tool in the hands of populists. What is populism in terms of its distinct political style? Palonen (2009) and Farrand and Carrapico (2021) argue that populism is rooted in antagonism, which considers society as "*ultimately separated*" into two homogeneous and hostile groups, that is "*the pure people versus the corrupt elite*" or "*those who are not with us, are against us*". It is worth recalling at this point that all three key narratives we identified in our qualitative analysis of the CETA discourse in Chap. 7 exhibit strong polarising features. Indeed, they appeal to antagonistic attitudes and usurp the exclusive right to interpret reality in a holistic and exclusive way. Farrand and Carrapico (2021, p. 6) propose a systematic look at political styles typical of populism and technocracy (see Table 8.1).

Table 8.1 Key characteristics of populist and technocratic styles

	Populist political style	*Populist political style*
Logic of argumentation	'Of and for the people'	'Rational problem solving'
Manner of communication	'Low' style, impassioned and emotive language	'High' style, disimpassioned and unemotive language
Central narrative and discursive framing	Crisis, rupture, threat	Stability, continuity, progress

Following these systematics and taking into account the "manner of communication", we learn that one of the manifestations of the populist narrative is the dominance of emotional over expert content. This lesson will be a building block of the media populism ratio presented in the next section of this chapter.

If we want to reflect upon media populism somehow, we must cope with the fundamental question of what is meant by "media" nowadays. Recently, with the advent of the internet and the digitalisation era, media use has become increasingly individualised and personalised (Valkenburg et al. 2016). The internet has revolutionised the model of mass communication in the modern world. Nonetheless, the Polish media market demonstrates a high level of concentration. Considering the indicators of viewership, audience, readership, and income distribution, the share of the four largest outfits typically exceeds 70% and, in some cases, reaches 90% in Poland.[1] According to the Gemius/PBI study conducted in January 2020,[2] among the big internet portals operating on a national scale, the Poles most often read news on WP, Onet, and the websites of Radio ZET and TVN24. In total, the top 10 include four media outlets with foreign capital, which had a total of nearly 29.4 million visitors in January 2021. In comparison, the remaining six websites with the Polish capital attracted 37.2 million users in the same time. The indicator of "universal reach of traditional media and access to the internet" stands at 46% in Poland (Klimkiewicz 2020).[3] There is a lower penetration of fixed-line broadband internet in Poland than the EU average (18.6% compared to 34.1 % in 2018).[4] It can therefore be assumed that major media outlets do play a significant role in shaping mass perception and that they are responsible for extremely suggestive and socially resonant framing.

In democratic states, where political pluralism makes it necessary to constantly communicate the positions, opinions, and attitudes between political actors, media are such actors. They do not only mediate in the process of communication but consciously take their own positions by agreeing with certain actors and disagreeing with others. In this situation,

[1] https://wiadomosci.dziennik.pl/media/artykuly/556651,koncentracja-mediow-pluralizm-media-finansowanie-abonament.html

[2] https://www.gemius.pl/wszystkie-artykuly-aktualnosci/wyniki-badania-gemiuspbi-za-styczen-2020.html

[3] https://cadmus.eui.eu/bitstream/handle/1814/67813/poland_results_mpm_2020_cmpf.pdf?sequence=1&isAllowed=y

[4] Ibid.

the attempt to consistently maintain impartiality towards politicians' views should be seen as an act of political self-determination.

The position of analysed outlets on Polish media landscape is determined on the one hand by their position on the main European public discussions (level of sovereignty of the EU member states, climate crisis, immigration, gender equality, etc.) and on the other hand by the images of the past that they tend to support and create in its audience (Stryjek 2021). The relative importance of historical issues in this context seems to be a specificity of Polish media landscape. Stryjek, who analysed the representation of history in media in Poland, divided the media outlets into three main categories according to the intensity of presenting ethnic nationalism. The most strongly attached to this idea would be right-wing outlets, while the left-wing ones would not only deny any forms of ethnic nationalism but be critical to any nationalism as a community-forming idea. Considering Stryjek's classification and adding the criteria of cultural and economic liberalism as discussed in Chap. 4, the media outlets analysed in this book can be positioned as presented in a table below.

The choice of media for analysis made by us was based first of all on the criteria of their popularity and impact on the shape of public discourse in Poland, but we also tried to ensure the representation of the whole spectrum of political-ideological orientations.

Applying Stryjek's classification, the portals analysed in Chaps. 6 and 7 can be positioned on the left-right scale as shown in Table 8.2.

Generally speaking it is not easy to give the media outlets political-ideological labels because the political or ideological flavour of published texts—if it exists at all—depends much on the author and the topic. The portal www.eurotopics.net[5] classifies the same media outlets differently than we do, but the criteria of their classification are not published. Economic issues, however, and Free Trade Agreements in particular seem

Table 8.2 Political-ideological orientation of the analysed media outlets

Left(liberal in cultural sense)		*Centrist(liberal in economic sense)*		*Right(conservative, nationalist)*
natemat.pl	gazeta.pl onet.pl	interia.pl	rp.pl wp.pl	fronda.pl

[5] Their political-ideological classification of some Polish media outlets—see https://bit.ly/3e5KMXN (accessed March 3rd, 2021)

to be the topic where it is quite natural to express the political position—especially on the scale of nationalism. We would expect the media that are "liberal in economic sense" present an approach closer to "technocratic political style" (Farrand & Carapico, 2021), presented in the following section.

8.2 Media Populism Ratio

Following Farrand and Carapico's (2021) definition of the populist political style (see Table 8.1), we postulate that more populist media outlets are marked by a higher level of emotional content relative to fact-based expert content. Therefore, we propose the Media Populism Ratio (MPR) defined as the share of emotional words within an article (based on the eight types of emotions discussed in Chap. 6) divided by the share of words belonging to the Expert Knowledge Dictionary developed in Chap. 5:

$$MPR = \frac{number\ of\ emotion-tagged\ words}{number\ of\ expert\ knowledge\ words}.$$

Using the same sample of online articles as in Chaps. 6 and 7, we calculate MPR on an article level for the whole sample of 2685 outputs. Table 8.3 shows summary statistics for the MPR's components as well as the ratio itself. The mean value of MPR stands at 6.13, which means that an average article contains over six times more emotionally loaded words.

The purpose of MPR is to identify which articles could be classified as populist. Unfortunately, we do not have any exogenous, absolutely objective, or independent yardstick that we could use as a threshold above which articles' character becomes populist. Instead, we need to base our ensuing considerations on the properties of our sample. As noted previously in this chapter and Chap. 6, our articles come from several internet portals that range in their ideological sentiment from the right-wing,

Table 8.3 Emotions, expert knowledge, and MPR

Variable	*Mean*	*Std. Dev.*	*Min*	*Max*
Emotional words (% of all words)	17.83	5.59	0	44.65
Expert words (% of all words)	5.9	3.42	0	18
MPR	6.13	10.53	0	185

through centrist to left-wing. Thus, we expect to have a fairly balanced sample. In practice, we identify populist articles as those whose MPR deviates upwards from the mean value by more than one standard deviation. More concisely written, an article *i* is populist if

$$MPR_i > \overline{MPR} + s_{MPR},$$

where MPR_i is the value of MPR for article *i*, $\overline{MPR}$ is the sample mean MPR (average across all articles) and s_{MPR} is the sample standard deviation of MPR values from the mean. We realise that our use of one standard deviation to calculate the benchmark is rather arbitrary, and therefore, we repeated our analysis with alternative values of 0.5 and two standard deviations. In each case, the relative rankings of articles and outlets' populism remained the same as those presented in Table 8.4 below. Furthermore, we have 19 articles that do not contain any expert terms, and therefore we cannot calculate their MPRs (as this would mean a division by zero). However, all of them are characterised by an above-average high share of emotional words, so in the ensuing discussion, we classify them as populist texts.

Using our criterion, we classify 206 out of 2685 articles as populist. This means that across the Polish internet media, one in 13 articles on FTAs contains much more emotional than expert content and therefore could be labelled as populist. Table 8.4 also shows how the values of MPR and share of populist articles rank across the respective media outlets.

We are not surprised to see that fronda.pl (classified by Stryjek 2021 as distinctly right-wing, conservative and nationalist media outlet) is at the

Table 8.4 Emotions, expert knowledge, and MPR

	Articles	*Average MPR*	*Articles identified as populist*	
			Number	*Share*
All outlets	2685	6.13	206	7.67%
fronda.pl	95	11.96	25	26.32%
wp.pl	354	8.92	57	16.1%
natemat.pl	91	8.16	11	12.09%
gazeta.pl	365	5.9	31	8.49%
onet.pl	743	5.76	45	6.06%
rp.pl	650	5.11	26	4%
interia.pl	368	4.21	11	2.99%

top of the ranking. It is also rather in line with our intuition that the media outlets perceived as centrist and liberal (in an economic sense) are mostly at the opposite end of the spectrum. Wp.pl, with its relatively high MPR and share of populist articles, appears to be an exception here. The relatively high populist content of wp.pl may be explained by its efforts to maintain neutral political position—not by staying outside of public debate but by giving voice to all sides of the political spectrum. One can read the opinions of well-known conservative journalists as well as the comments by leftist or liberal ones on wp.pl. Sometimes they debate with each other, which encourages using emotional language.

Recent years have been marked by resurgence of populist politics in many countries across the globe, including the US, the UK, Italy, the Philippines, Brazil, and Poland. This process can be likely traced back to the Great Recession of 2008 and the ensuing economic turbulences as well as the migration crises that affected many countries in Europe and the US. Thus, our next step is to investigate whether this rise of populist politics finds its reflection in our media content. To achieve this, we compare the percentage share of populist articles in all articles published before the end of 2008 with the analogous indicator calculated for the period from 2009 onward. Indeed, we observe a dramatic jump in the relative frequency of populist articles. Until 2008, only 2.7% of the analysed texts could be classified as populist, whereas this value increased to 8.86% in the period between 2009 and 2019. Thus, the share of populist articles in the FTA-related Polish online media content more than tripled after the Great Recession. This can be partly explained by the emergence and increasing popularity of the two ideologically-marked outlets, fronda.pl and natemat.pl, which rank highly in the populist content (see Table 8.4), but this supply-side explanation is only a part of the story.

8.3 Summarising Remarks

Building on the content of the previous chapters, we proposed a measure of media populism: (MPR) and we find it quite a useful tool that helps to identify (compare) the populist media content

Relying on the MPR, we are capable of providing evidence of the populism rise after the GFC. We show that "ideologically-driven" outlets which seek to appeal either to the right or to the left side of the political spectrum are more likely to publish populist content.

There are some shortcomings in our approach. Our measure takes into consideration only two dimensions: emotions and expert knowledge, which are notoriously difficult to measure, and their measurement may depend on the context. It might be blind to graphical cues (layout of certain websites and portals) as well as the type of photographs published—what emotions are they intended to invoke? How much do they try to shock, anger? As communication channels and their use change over time, so may the content of a typical message. Thus, it is possible that we learned to communicate more emotions over recent years, and thus intertemporal comparisons of MPR may be problematic.

References

Brzeziński, M. (2017). Is high inequality an issue in Poland?. Institute Badań Strukturalnych Policy Paper, 6.

Brzezinski, Michal, and Katarzyna Salach. "Why wealth inequality differs between post-socialist countries?." Available at SSRN 3631191 (2020).

Brzezinski, M., Salach, K., & Wroński, M. (2019). Wealth inequality in Central and Eastern Europe: evidence from joined household survey and rich lists' data. *Available at SSRN 3497399.*

Iyengar, Shanto, Yphtach Lelkes, Matthew Levendusky, Neil Malhotra, and Sean J. Westwood. 2019. 'The Origins and Consequences of Affective Polarization in the United States.' Annual Review of Political Science.

Klimkiewicz, B. (2020). Monitoring media pluralism in the digital era: application of the Media Pluralism Monitor 2020 in the European Union, Albania & Turkey: country report: Poland.

Levendusky, Matthew. 2018. 'Americans, Not Partisans: Can Priming American National Identity Reduce Affective Polarization?' The Journal of Politics 80(1), 59-70

Levendusky, M., & Malhotra, N. (2016). Does media coverage of partisan polarization affect political attitudes?. *Political Communication*, *33*(2), 283-301.

Lonergan, E., & Blyth, M. (2020). Angrynomics, Agenda Publishing.

Palonen, E. (2009). Political polarisation and populism in contemporary Hungary. Parliamentary Affairs, 62(2), 318-334.

Reiljan, A. (2020). 'Fear and loathing across party lines' (also) in Europe: Affective polarisation in European party systems. European journal of political research, 59(2), 376-396.

Stryjek, T. (2021), Rzeczpospolita podzieolona. Obrazy przeszłości i dyskursy historyczne w prasie polskiej w 2018 r. Próba zmapowania debaty, w: Barbara Markowska (red.), Reprezentacje przeszłości w polskiej i ukraińskiej sferze medialnej, Wyd. Naukowe Scholar: Warszawa, in print.

Tworzecki, H. (2019). Poland: a case of top-down polarisation. The ANNALS of the American Academy of Political and Social Science, 681(1), 97-119.

Valkenburg, P. M., Peter, J., & Walther, J. B. (2016). Media effects: Theory and research. *Annual review of psychology*, *67*, 315-338.

Index[1]

[1] Note: Page numbers followed by 'n' refer to notes.

B. Gawrońska-Nowak et al., *Trade Wins or Trade Wars*,
https://doi.org/10.1007/978-3-030-76997-0